CREATIVE THERAPY:
52 EXERCISES FOR GROUPS

Jane Dossick & Eugene Shea

Illustrated by Eugene Shea

Professional Resource Exchange, Inc.
Sarasota, Florida

This book was produced in the USA using a patented European binding technology called Ota-bind. We chose this unique binding because it allows pages to lay flat for photocopying, is stronger than standard bindings for this purpose, and has numerous advantages over spiral-binding (e.g., less chance of damage in shipping, no unsightly spiral marks on photocopies, and a spine you can read when the book is on your bookshelf).

Printed in the United States of America

ISBN: 0-943158-50-8
Library of Congress Catalog Number: 88-42577

The copy editor for this book was Judy Warinner, the production supervisor was Debbie Fink, the graphics coordinator was Carol Hirsch, and the cover designer was Bill Tabler.

For Joanne, Philip, and Stephen

TABLE OF CONTENTS

INTRODUCTION

WHO SHOULD USE THIS BOOK?

Creative Therapy: 52 Exercises for Groups was designed as a practical guide to assist psychotherapists, group leaders, and specially trained teachers in mental health facilities, nursing homes, day programs, inpatient psychiatric units, special education programs, and support groups. It may be used as an adjunct to the psychotherapeutic treatment of such varied problems as Alzheimer's disease, schizophrenia, mental retardation, and depression.

This how-to book contains 52 therapeutic exercises complete with illustrations that may be photocopied for group members. For both new and experienced group leaders, this book explains methods of energizing a group, and takes the reader through the stages for effective implementation of these structured exercises. We have been successfully using these original materials for many years in a major New York City long-term care hospital. We find that these exercises can help group members develop interactive skills, motivate less verbal individuals to contribute to group discussions, and encourage group cohesiveness. The exercise serves as an avenue to therapeutic discussions of important issues that might not be reached through other techniques.

WHAT IS IN THIS BOOK?

Creative Therapy: 52 Exercises for Groups is presented in an uncomplicated fashion so that the exercises will be nonthreatening to group members. The format allows the leader to refer to directions for each group meeting, and photocopy the accompanying illustration, which becomes each members' worksheet. In each exercise members complete a picture that focuses on a particular theme. A discussion follows in which the members discuss what their completed pictures reveal about themselves. The illustrations are intentionally simple to encourage participants to express themselves as freely as possible.

HOW DO YOU USE THIS BOOK?

Creative Therapy: 52 Exercises for Groups takes structured exercises for groups beyond the usual verbal techniques. The worksheet provided with each exercise serves as a springboard to discussion for group members. Each exercise is accompanied by a step-by-step set of instructions for the group leader.

Group members sit at a table, preferably in a circle. The leader hands out photocopies of the chosen exercise to members at the beginning of the session. The leader should seek to involve members immediately by asking about the picture.

The group leader introduces the theme, describes the exercise according to the instructions that accompany each drawing, and asks for feedback and comments from the group members. This initial discussion should be used to prepare the members for the task that follows.

Next, group members are given a time frame and directed to "fill in" or complete the exercise with their responses. Additional supplies such as crayons, markers, or pencils may be handed out at this time.

It is important to be certain everyone has a clear understanding of the task. If questions are asked, it is recommended that members be encouraged to ask each other to paraphrase the instructions. In this way members are kept actively involved and can be helpful to one another.

Setting up a time frame is an important aspect of the structured exercise. These projects work best if the group members understand how much time is set aside for drawing, and how much time is for discussion. For example, in a 1 hour group, 20 minutes might be used for explanation and drawing, and 40 minutes for discussion.

These exercises should be nonthreatening. To reduce anxiety, group leaders should explain that content is more important than artistic talent. The drawings are used to promote discussion. Some members may be resistant to drawing because of self-consciousness or physical limitations. Encouragement is helpful, but too much encouragement may become stressful. An alternative is to avoid adding extra pressure by allowing anxious members to write rather than draw their interpretations.

Group discussion immediately follows the drawing period. The leader should state a few minutes ahead of time when this will take place. Once group discussion begins, all members' comments should then be directed to the group as a whole.

Members are asked to volunteer to discuss their interpretations. The leader becomes a catalyst to promote and encourage verbal interaction, and to help focus the discussion. As members see one another present and receive feedback, more may volunteer to discuss their work.

WHAT ARE THE BENEFITS?

Projective art tasks introduce ideas that provide encouragement to groups searching for a common theme (Dalley, 1984). In addition, these structured exercises have a variety of other uses: to initiate members into a group process; as a warm-up technique; to help a group work through a particular stage in its development; to enhance group members' abilities to interact and share freely; to focus on a specific group need; and to help reduce group members' anxiety and uncertainty. It must be understood however, that they are intended as a tool - as one part of a total approach to meet the goals of a particular group.

Structured exercises are a way of accelerating group interaction. Getting in touch with suppressed emotions helps the group as a whole as well as the individual members. Specific exercises may be chosen to help the group work through a particular problem (Hansen, Warner, & Smith, 1980).

Yalom (1983) describes the use of structured exercises with lower-level, inpatient psychotherapy groups. These groups often consist of members with a limited attention span, fearfulness, and confusion. Structured exercises may help such members express themselves. The use of art or drawing exercises is especially helpful in fostering self-expression. These exercises may also stimulate group interest and provide variety. We believe the exercises in *Creative Therapy: 52 Exercises for Groups* are very effective with this type of group.

Structured exercises also help insure that no one dominates, that everyone has an opportunity to speak. A balance of verbal input is created. Monopolistic members must develop self-control to allow other members to have their turns. Shy or nonverbal members profit from the required participation, such as described by Levin and Kurtz (1974). The authors studied the effects of structured exercises in human relations groups and concluded that the inactive person benefits from a change in behavioral expectations. Greater opportunity for participation generates more ego-involvement, self-perceived personality changes, and increased group unity.

How does group therapy help group members? Feedback from one's peers, if properly channeled, can be a potent therapeutic force, promoting qualitative changes in self-expression, growth toward self-actualization, and changes in interpersonal behavior.

In his classic work on group psychotherapy, Yalom identifies key curative factors associated with the group process. We believe that many of the exercises included in this book facilitate the curative process. Generally, the exercises encourage sharing and development of trust among group members. The drawings illustrate common fears and anxieties and allow group members to see how each of them share many of the same concerns. Through the use of the illustrations, members are encouraged to support each other's needs and find solutions to problems. Skilled therapists will strategically use the exercises to support the development of other curative factors within the group.

WHAT ARE THE LIMITATIONS
OF THESE EXERCISES?

Through experience, we have found these exercises and materials to be of value. It is important, however, to realize the limitations of their use as well. As we have said, these exercises are to be used as a springboard to discussion; as an adjunct to other therapies.

Yalom (1985) describes possible negative effects structured exercises can have on groups. He suggests, for example, that they can create an atmosphere where critical stages of group interaction may be passed over. Structured exercises may also plunge the group members into sharing significant negative and positive feelings too quickly. In addition, the group leader may be too heavily relied upon by the members. This dissipates the group's potential effectiveness as a therapeutic agent.

The Lieberman, Yalom, and Miles encounter group project (1973) studied how structured exercises influence groups. The leaders who used relatively large numbers of structured exercises with their groups were often more popular with group members. These same group members were found to have a significantly lower outcome level than members participating in groups using fewer structured exercises.

There must be a balance to the use of structured exercises. The degree to which they should be used must be carefully weighed by the group leader, otherwise the leader runs the risk of reducing the group's potential, and infantilizing the members. Some factors that determine the amount and type of structuring to be employed are the type of group, member characteristics, and the leader's theoretical orientation (M. S. Corey & G. Corey, 1987).

Additionally, the group leader should keep in mind three of the considerations noted by Pfeiffer and Jones (1983). First, structured exercises should address the specific goals and purposes of the group. The leader should choose exercises directed at interest, concerns, or problems of individual members or of the group as a whole. Second, a more than casual understanding of the members is important, because revelation and exploration of fantasy can be threatening and anxiety-provoking. Less threatening exercises are recommended for groups with anxious or guarded members to promote openness rather than defensiveness. Third, different issues surface at various stages of group development. Groups will function best when the level of feedback expected corresponds to the developmental stage of the group. In early stages of group development, exercises that focus on openness and building trust are more appropriate. Exercises that focus on critical feedback and appraisal will be more successful in the later stages of group development.

CONCLUSION

Creative Therapy: 52 Exercises for Groups is rewarding to both the group leader and the group members. The structured exercises in this book make it easier for group members to focus ideas, feelings, and experiences related to the topic of discussion. Members further benefit from revealing themselves, exchanging feedback, and supporting one another emotionally.

The purpose of this book, however, is first and foremost to help group leaders, therapists, and teachers conduct their groups by providing a framework for successful group experiences.

Through the use of specific suggestions, we describe the procedures necessary for group leaders to handle the widest variety of group therapy applications. In addition, the use of these exercises may also help to alert group leaders to issues for further exploration in individual counseling or other group therapies.

REFERENCES

Corey, M. S., & Corey, G. (1987). *Groups: Process & Practice* (3rd ed.). Monterey, CA: Brooks/Cole.

Dalley, T. (1984). *Art As Therapy: An Introduction to the Use of Art As a Therapeutic Technique.* New York: Tavistock.

Hansen, J. C., Warner, R. W., & Smith, E. J. (1980). *Group Counseling: Theory and Process* (2nd ed.). Chicago: Rand McNally.

Levin, E. N., & Kurtz, R. R. (1974). Structured and non structured human relations training. *Journal of Counseling Psychology, 21,* 526-531.

Lieberman, M. A., Yalom, I. D., & Miles, M. B. (1973). *Encounter Groups: First Facts.* New York: Basic Books.

Pfeiffer, J. W., & Jones, J. E. (1983). *A Handbook of Structured Experiences for Human Relations Training: Reference Guide to Hand Books and Annuals.* San Diego: University Associates.

Shulman, L. (1979). *The Skills of Helping Individuals and Groups.* Itasca, IL: Peacock Publications.

Yalom, I. D. (1983). *Inpatient Group Psychotherapy.* New York: Basic Books.

Yalom, I. D. (1985). *The Theory and Practice of Group Psychotherapy* (3rd ed.). New York: Basic Books.

CREATIVE THERAPY:
52 EXERCISES
FOR GROUPS

Exercise 1

THE PATH

Purpose:

1. To provide the opportunity for self-disclosure.
2. To share fantasies in order to promote heightened awareness of self and others.

Materials:

One photocopy of the illustration for each member; crayons or markers.

Description:

A. The group leader asks members to explore the reasons different places appeal to different people.
B. While handing out the materials, the leader describes this exercise as an opportunity for members to show the group a place they've been to or would like to visit.
C. Each member is told to draw himself or herself on the path.
D. Members draw in a traveling companion (this other person may be someone from the past or the present).

Group Discussion:

Members are encouraged to reveal themselves by describing their drawing. The group is engaged in a discussion of what the choice of destination and companion reveal about each member. Some members may describe an imagined destination.

Often, this exercise evolves into a reminiscence group, as members tell about an actual place they have visited or lived in. The leader encourages members to question and comment about related events and feelings.

It is interesting to explore the personal qualities of the chosen traveling companion. Is it someone the group member is close to, or would like to be close to?

The self-revelation involved in this exercise is relatively nonthreatening. This makes it appropriate for groups in the early stages of development.

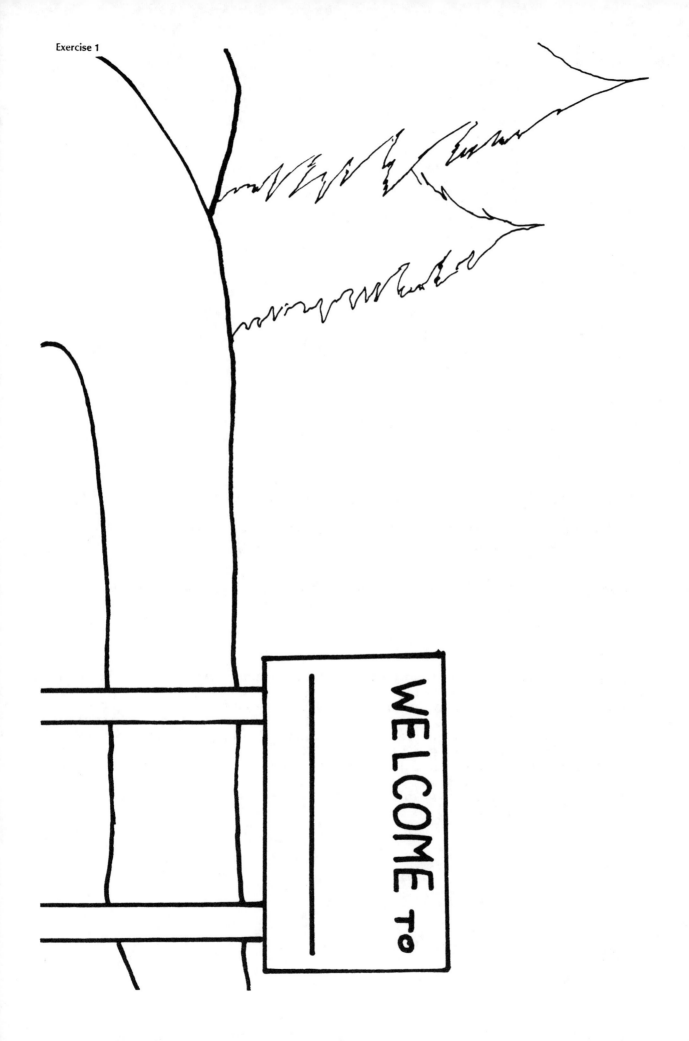

Exercise 2

TIME MACHINE

Purpose:

1. To share memories and compare experiences.
2. To promote empathy.
3. To incorporate group feedback into self-evaluation.

Materials:

One photocopy of the illustration for each member; crayons or markers.

Description:

A. The leader asks the group to talk about the fantasy of living life over and doing things differently.
B. While handing out the materials, the leader tells members to imagine returning to a time in their lives that they would like to change.
C. The group is told to draw the event not as it really happened, but how it might have been if things were different.
D. Members include what they should have done to achieve this altered past.

Group Discussion:

First, each member shares the actual past event or experience. Then they reveal how they changed the past. Empathy is promoted by encouraging others to understand why each person would have preferred the changed event or experience. Members are encouraged to give advice on other ways they could have changed the past.

This exercise is most effective with groups that are well integrated, and able to benefit from critical feedback.

Variation:

Members choose a positive period in their life that they would like to relive. Group discussion and feedback focuses on understanding the significance of those events.

"TIME MACHINE"

Exercise 3

CARTOON

Purpose:

1. To promote interpersonal learning through sharing constructive responses to negative experiences.
2. To recognize feelings as a response to the environment.

Materials:

One photocopy of the illustration for each member; pens or pencils.

Description:

A. The group begins the exercise by discussing the benefits of listening, of giving advice, and of understanding why we have certain feelings.
B. While handing out the materials, group members are told that they will be filling in the word balloons on cartoons.
C. In the first two cartoons, members give advice on how to deal with difficult feelings.
D. The last two cartoons are more personal and request the members to share insight about their own feelings.

Group Discussion:

Each member reads their cartoon to the group. Members describe why they recommend particular responses to specific negative situations. The group is encouraged to give feedback. Members also tell why certain experiences make them fearful, happy, or unhappy. The group comments on what this reveals about each person. Common themes emerge, and are focused upon. This exercise is most effective with groups that are capable of sharing insight.

Exercise 4

THE GARBAGE PAIL

Purpose:

1. To encourage empathy through identification with the feelings of others.
2. To present risk-taking through revealing negative aspects of a person's own life.
3. To recognize common themes in order to illustrate that many problems are universal.

Materials:

One photocopy of the illustration for each member; crayons or markers.

Description:

A. The group leader holds up the illustration and asks the group what they think the garbage pail symbolizes. The leader directs the discussion towards a focus on having the opportunity to throw something out of their lives.
B. While handing out the materials, the leader tells members to imagine discarding something. This may be a person, an object, a place, or a feeling.
C. They are told to illustrate this as if it were being dropped from the hand to the wastebasket.

Group Discussion:

Members describe the negative aspects of their lives as presented in their illustrations. The group explores individual choices through comments and questions. The leader helps the group to identify feelings and common themes. Some people will identify tangible disappointments, such as a useless gift. Others will describe abstract concepts such as entering a poor relationship.

Leaders may often find that members discard the negative aspects of the environment in which they are living. This is especially true for inpatient or residential facilities. This exercise works well with almost any group type in any stage of development because of its wide range of acceptable responses (person, object, place, or feeling). In addition, it may be useful in acquainting new members with one another in the early stage of group development.

Variation:

The sheet is turned upside-down as if something were being dropped from the basket into the hand. The exercise would focus on describing something (person, object, place, or feeling) members would like to retrieve which they had discarded in the past.

Exercise 5

THE BIRTHDAY CAKE

Purpose:

1. To share fantasies in order to promote greater awareness of self.
2. To explore the needs of others through the expression of their wishes and desires.

Materials:

One photocopy of the illustration for each member; crayons or markers.

Description:

A. The group leader introduces the theme of wishing. Members discuss the importance of wishing in their lives.
B. While handing out the materials, group members are told to focus on any desires or wishes they would like fulfilled.
C. In the space provided, they draw a wish as if it were being made on their birthday.

Group Discussion:

Members share their wishes and describe why they made them. The leader encourages group members to tell what they think is revealed about each person. Members are encouraged to comment further about additional wishes they feel each person should make to fulfill his or her needs. Positive feelings will usually emerge as the discussion progresses.

This exercise is nonthreatening. It can be used with any group type at any stage of development. A birthday wish is something just about everyone can relate to.

Variation:

Members illustrate a past wish that came true. Group discussion and feedback focuses on understanding the significance of that experience.

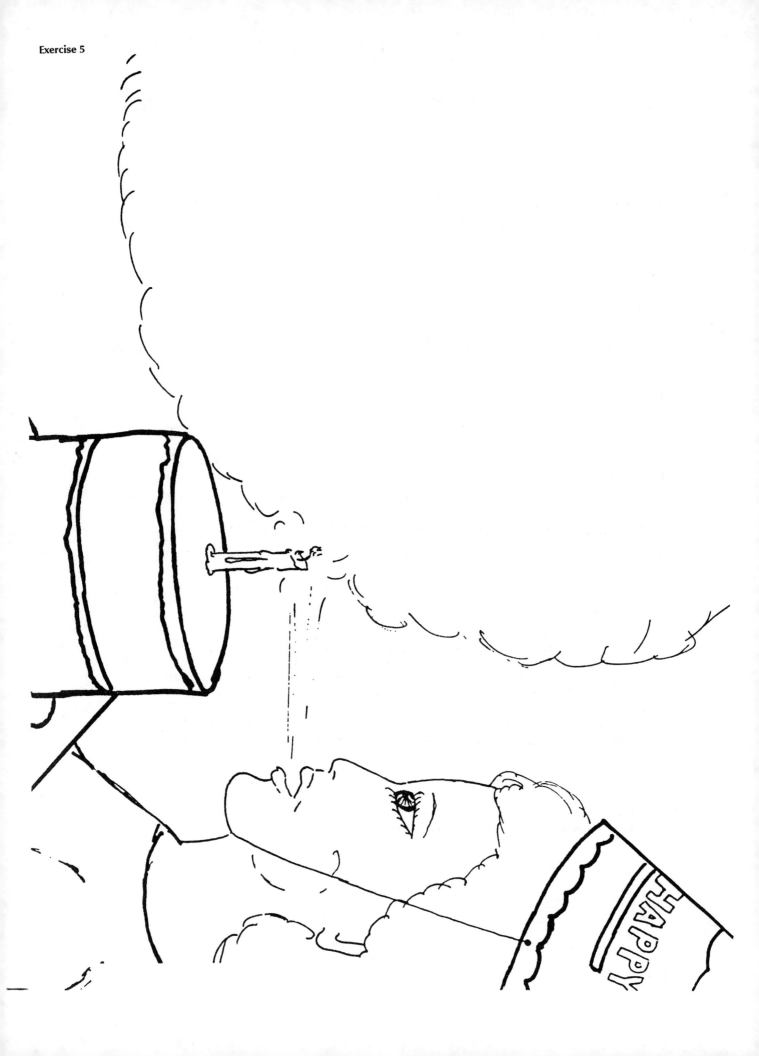

Exercise 6

COMING ATTRACTIONS AT THE MOVIES

Purpose:

1. To reveal self-image through fantasy.
2. To allow participants to receive feedback in a nonthreatening way.
3. To explore imagination in order to arrive at generalized perceptions about oneself.

Materials:

One photocopy of the illustration for each member; crayons or markers.

Description:

A. The group members discuss how the fantasy of being a movie star represents both fame and the opportunity to become anyone they would like to be.
B. While handing out the materials, the leader asks members to imagine the type of movie they would like to star in and what role they would choose.
C. Members are told to draw in the scene that best depicts their role and the type of movie (i.e., comedy, horror, romance, etc.).
D. Additionally, the members are told to include the scenery and an appropriate title for their movie.

Group Discussion:

Members share their drawings with the group, and tell why they chose to star in their particular type of movie and to portray their character. Members discuss whether they visualize their fellow members in their movie.

The leader helps the group explore why some members have illustrated movies that accurately portray themselves, while others chose characters and settings that enhanced their self-image.

Group members often add constructively to the discussion, commenting on the personal strengths and qualities of each member.

This exercise should be used by groups in which members are well-acquainted with each other.

WE'RE ALL IN THE SAME BOAT

Purpose:

1. To demonstrate universality through the recognition of common problems.
2. To promote group identity and cohesion by bonding together and being supportive of one another.

Materials:

The group leader photocopies one copy of the bow and stern of the boat to be given to two members; then the leader photocopies as many midsections as the remaining number of participants. The leader hands out crayons or markers. Adhesive tape will be needed at the end of the group session.

Description:

A. The leader asks the group to comment on what is meant by the saying "We're all in the same boat."
B. Members are each given a section of the boat and told to illustrate one problem they feel they have in common with other group members.
C. Before discussion begins, the leader collects the illustrations and forms one long boat using adhesive tape.

Group Discussion:

Starting at one end of the boat, the leader asks each group member to describe the illustrated problem. The leader encourages feedback when each problem is presented, such as recognition of similar problems. Discussion focuses on mutual support and ways in which members can bond together to cope with common problems.

Members often share feelings about social or environmental limitations, such as conflict with staff or administrative policy, discord with each other, and dietary restrictions.

This exercise is effective with groups beyond the early stages of development.

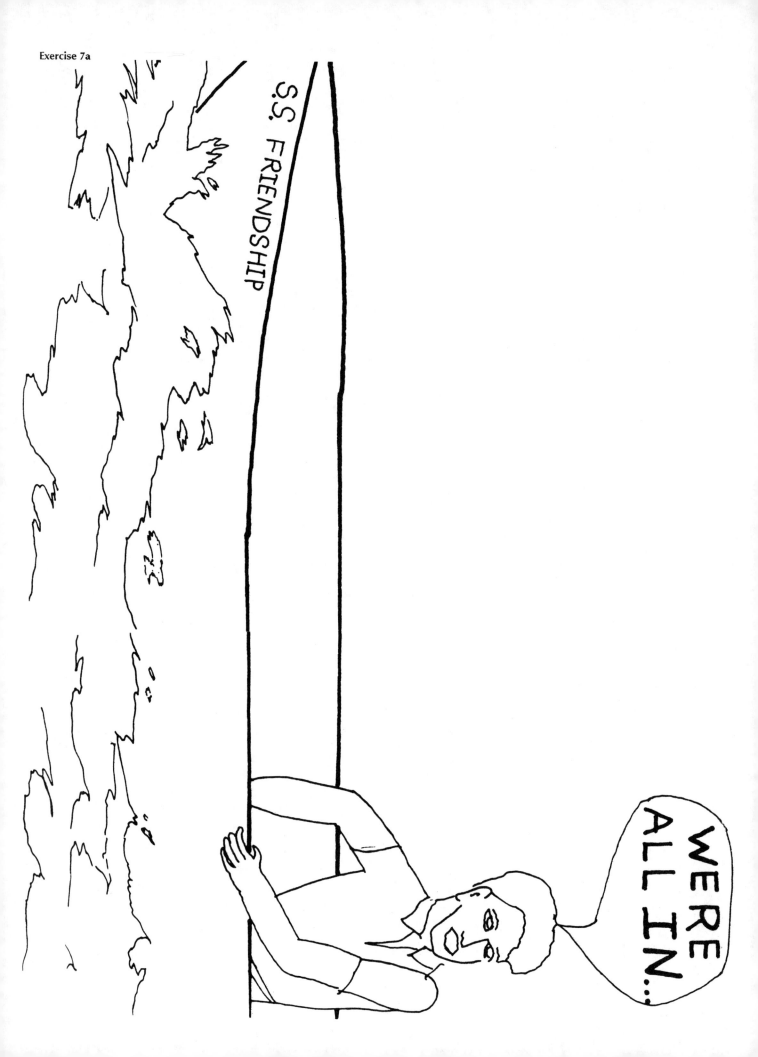

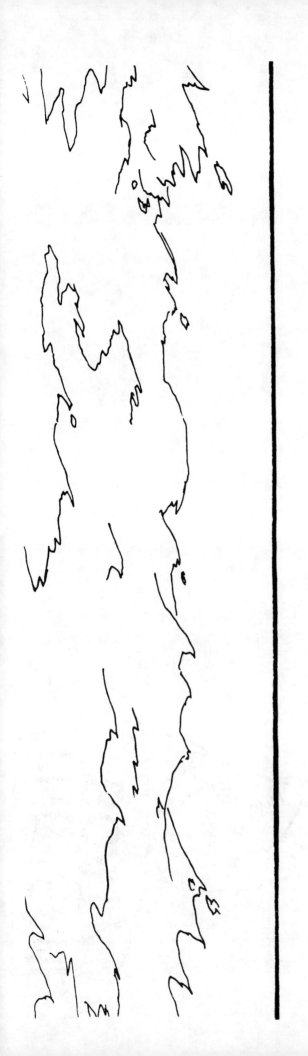

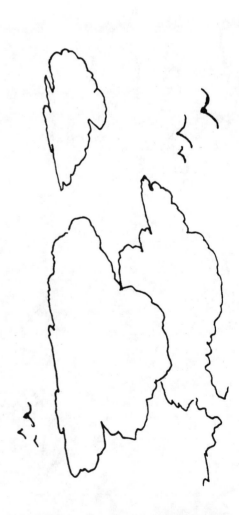

Exercise 8

THE WINDOW

Purpose:

1. To provide an opportunity to clarify feelings about what is missing from members' lives.
2. To compare life experiences in order to learn more about each other.
3. To give and receive advice in order to better adjust to life situations.

Materials:

One photocopy of the illustration for each member; crayons or markers.

Description:

A. The leader shows the illustration to the group and asks for feedback about what it could represent.
B. While handing out materials, the leader incorporates the group ideas into a description of this illustration as a window to the outside world.
C. Members draw what they think they are missing that might be going on outside of the building.

Group Discussion:

Members describe what they are missing, and the leader asks them to include their feelings about this. The group is engaged in a discussion about what is revealed about each member. Members share their own experiences, positive or negative, related to the illustration. Group members often describe people they miss and places where they would prefer to be.

This exercise works best with inpatients and residents who often feel separated from the outside world. It also works well in the early stages of group development to help members get acquainted with each other.

Variation:

Participants describe what they fear outside of the window.

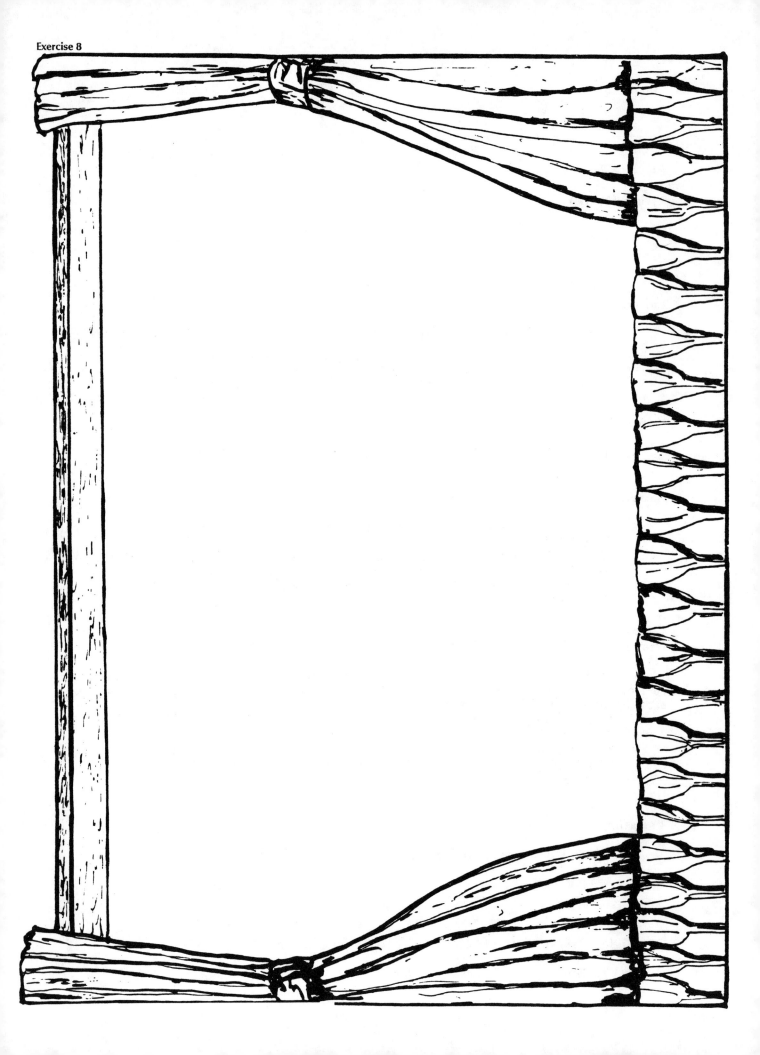

Exercise 9

MY PROBLEM

Purpose:

1. To allow members to communicate individual concerns in a nonthreatening way.
2. To develop individual and group problem-solving skills.
3. To reassure members that they can help each other.

Materials:

Each member will need a copy of the problem sheet and the answer sheet; crayons and pens or pencils.

Description:

A. The leader introduces the theme of how and why fellow members can effectively help solve each other's problems. Comments from the group are encouraged.
B. While giving out the problem sheet, the leader provides an overview of what this exercise entails.
C. Members illustrate and describe one problem on the corresponding sheet. The leader assures members that by not signing their names, the problems will remain anonymous.
D. The problem sheets are collected and redistributed at random. The blank answer sheet is also given out at this time.
E. Group members are told to illustrate or write their solutions to the anonymous problems.

Group Discussion:

Each member discusses his or her pair of illustrations, problems, and answers. Members should be encouraged to offer additional solutions.

Although some members may identify their own problems, the leader should discourage the group from guessing whose problem is being discussed.

In all stages of development, especially newly formed groups, anxiety over self-disclosure can be reduced through the anonymity provided by this exercise.

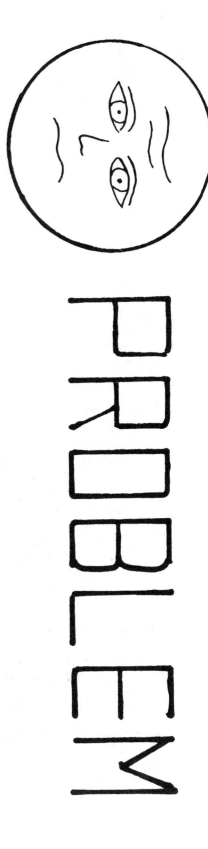

ANSWER

Exercise 10

OFF TO WORK

Purpose:

1. To recognize personal strengths and weaknesses.
2. To incorporate group feedback into self-evaluation.

Materials:

One photocopy of the illustration for each member; crayons or markers.

Description:

A. The group members are asked to describe what skills might be needed for a variety of jobs.
B. While handing out materials, the leader asks members to think about the type of job which might best suit them (not necessarily a job they have actually had).
C. Members illustrate this imagined job in the space provided.

Group Discussion:

Before each member shows his or her illustration, the leader asks others in the group to guess what kind of job has been chosen. Then each member reveals the job which has been illustrated.

The leader encourages members to question each other about why they chose their jobs. This exercise is designed for groups in which members are well-acquainted with each other's strengths and weaknesses.

Variation:

Members describe (if applicable) the types of jobs they had in the past. This variation works well with groups with limited abilities to think abstractly.

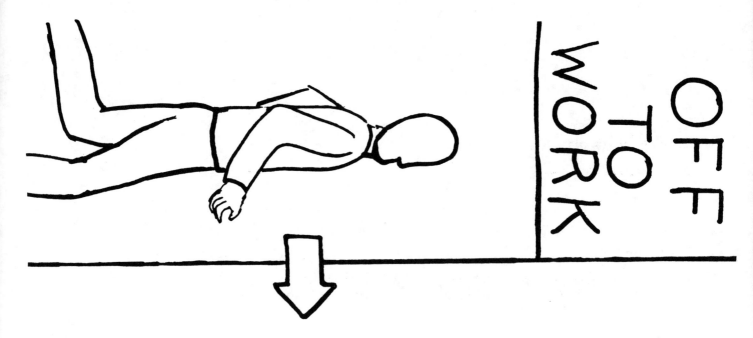

Exercise 11

THE X-RAY

Purpose:

1. To present risk-taking as a way of building trust.
2. To develop group cohesion through mutual self-disclosure.
3. To increase understanding and acceptance among members.

Materials:

One photocopy of the illustration for each member; crayons or markers.

Description:

A. The group discusses the theme of trusting others enough to be able to share hidden thoughts.
B. While handing out the materials, the leader tells group members to imagine an X-ray machine that can reveal people's secrets.
C. Each group member is told to draw or write on the X-ray screen one secret which he or she is willing to share with others.

Group Discussion:

Members reveal what appears on their X-ray screens. The leader encourages them to tell the others why these secrets are important to them. In turn, the members are encouraged to ask follow-up questions to gain a broader understanding of each other's secrets.

This exercise is effective with groups that can think abstractly, and are in the later stages of development.

X-RAY DEPT.

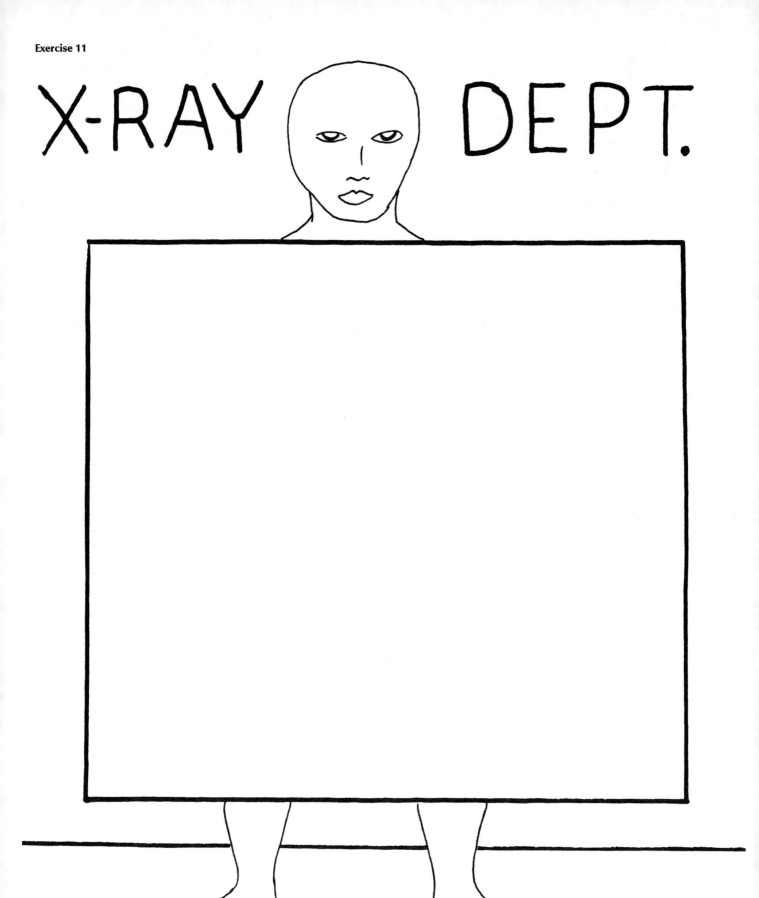

Exercise 12

TIME AND PLACE

Purpose:

1. To promote group identity.
2. To use teamwork in the development of shared decision making and task performance.
3. To focus on a given theme.

Materials:

Two photocopies of the illustration; crayons or markers.

Description:

A. The group begins this exercise by talking about common needs and experiences that they share which occur in places such as dining rooms, recreation rooms, and so on.
B. The group is divided into two teams that will operate independently.
C. Each team gets the illustration, then is told to choose a room or place they share in common. They are also told to choose day or night, and a season of the year.
D. Each team chooses one person to fill in the illustration.
E. The team members then discuss among themselves what this room or place would look like in the time period chosen. They are encouraged to add such things as people, furnishings, and so forth. The illustrator draws in what the team decides.

Group Discussion:

Each team shares its illustration, describing the room or place chosen, the time of day, the season, and what is happening. The leader explores with the group the feelings they had working as a team. Additionally, they discuss why certain members were chosen as illustrators and who emerged as the leader of each team.

We have observed that issues which arise often relate to the discontent members share about places in common. When this occurs, the group leader may help members to suggest appropriate resolutions, if possible.

This exercise is most effective with residents or inpatients, since they share many rooms in common.

Exercise 12

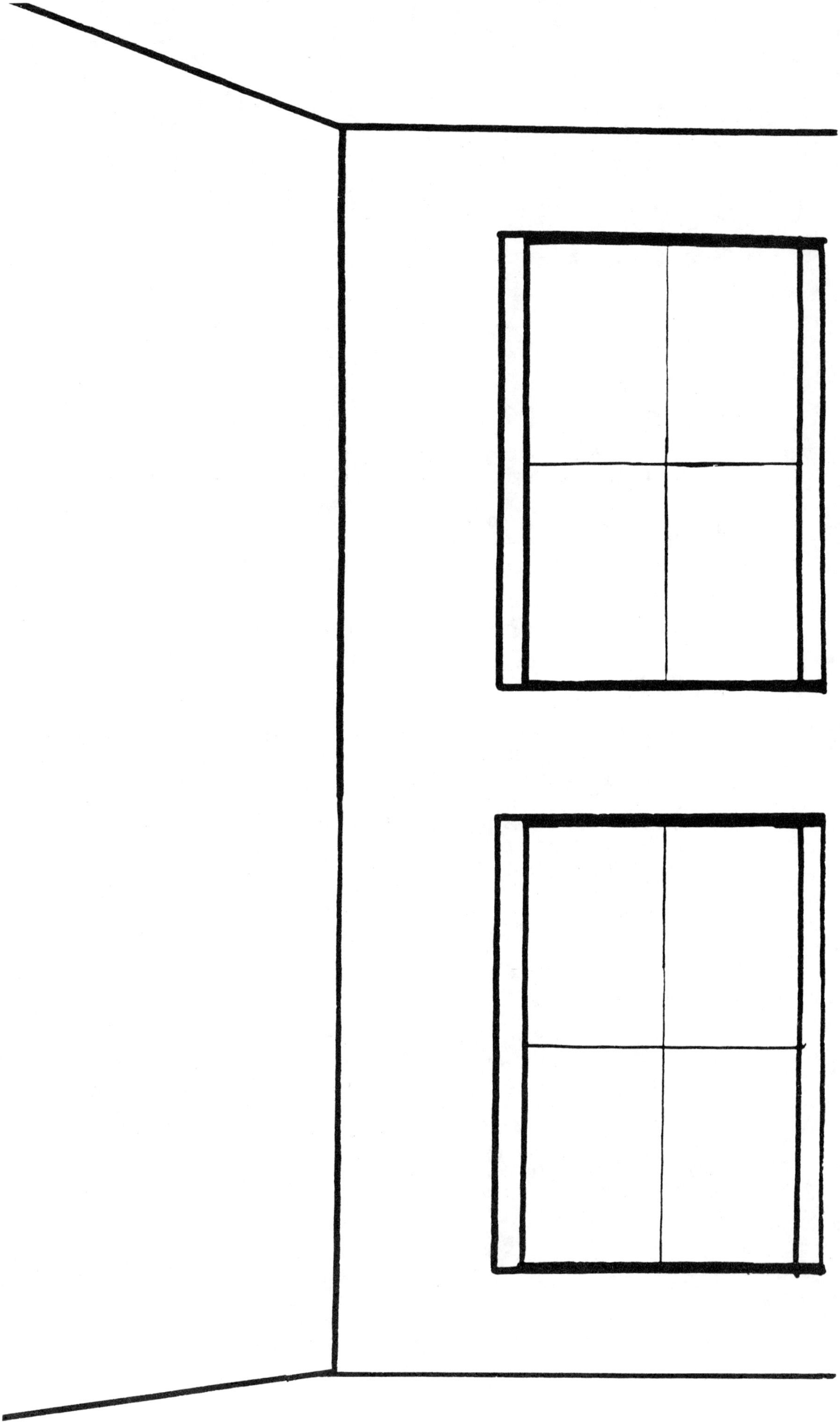

Exercise 13

THE GRASS IS GREENER

Purpose:

1. To provide an opportunity to clarify feelings about what is missing from members' lives.
2. To encourage empathy in order to better understand each other's needs.
3. To give and receive advice in order to better adjust to life situations.

Materials:

One photocopy of the illustration for each member; crayons or markers.

Description:

A. The leader asks the group to discuss the meaning of the saying "The grass is always greener on the other side of the fence." The materials are then distributed.
B. Members think of an unhappy situation in their lives, and draw it on one side of the fence.
C. On the other side of the fence, they illustrate ways other people seem to be better off.

Group Discussion:

Each member tells why he or she is unhappy with the chosen situation, and describes how others seem to be better off. The rest of the group is encouraged to ask questions and offer suggestions about how better to adjust to these unsatisfactory situations.

Though this exercise focuses on an individual member's less rewarding life situation, it may lead other members to help the individual concentrate on some more positive aspects of life, that had not been thought of previously.

This exercise works well with a wide variety of groups, in all stages of development.

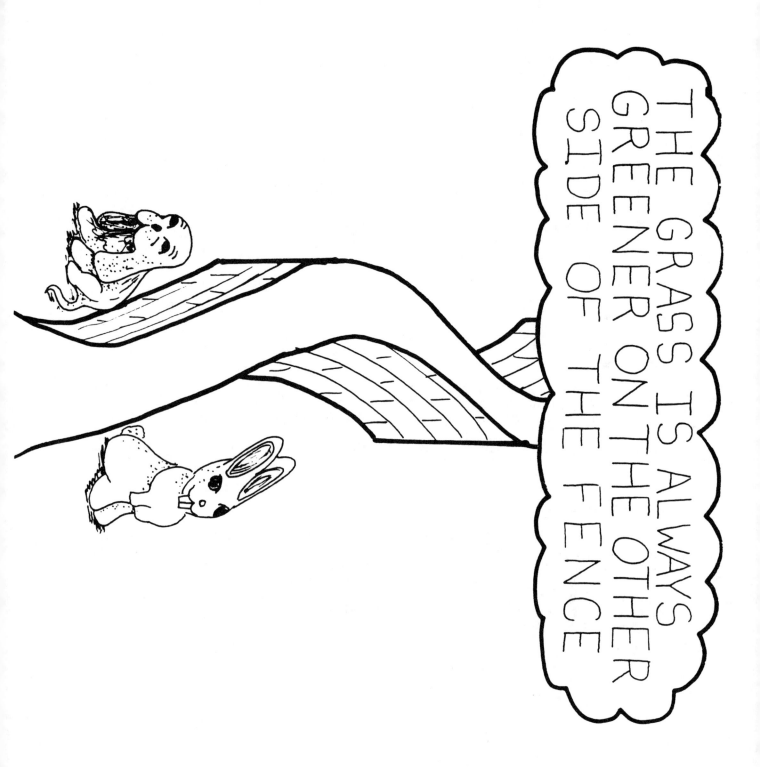

Exercise 14

THE GUEST

Purpose:

1. To explore what qualities attract one person to others.
2. To reinforce group socialization skills through simulated interpersonal conversation.

Materials:

One photocopy of the illustration for each member; crayons or markers.

Description:

A. The illustration is shown to the group. Members are asked to comment on what they think they will be asked to do in this exercise.
B. While handing out materials, the leader tells the members to think about dining with a guest. This may be someone they know, or could be someone they would like to get to know.
C. Members draw themselves, their guest, and the meal.
D. In the word balloons above the table, they write the imagined conversation.

Group Discussion:

Members tell why they chose their dinner guest. The leader helps them focus on what they find interesting about that person. Members describe the dinner, read the conversation, and expand upon it. The group leader encourages others to ask for more specific information about the guest, meal, and conversation.

Members often choose each other as their guests. Frequently they will talk about favorite foods and recipes.

This exercise may be used with a variety of groups in any stage of development.

Exercise 14

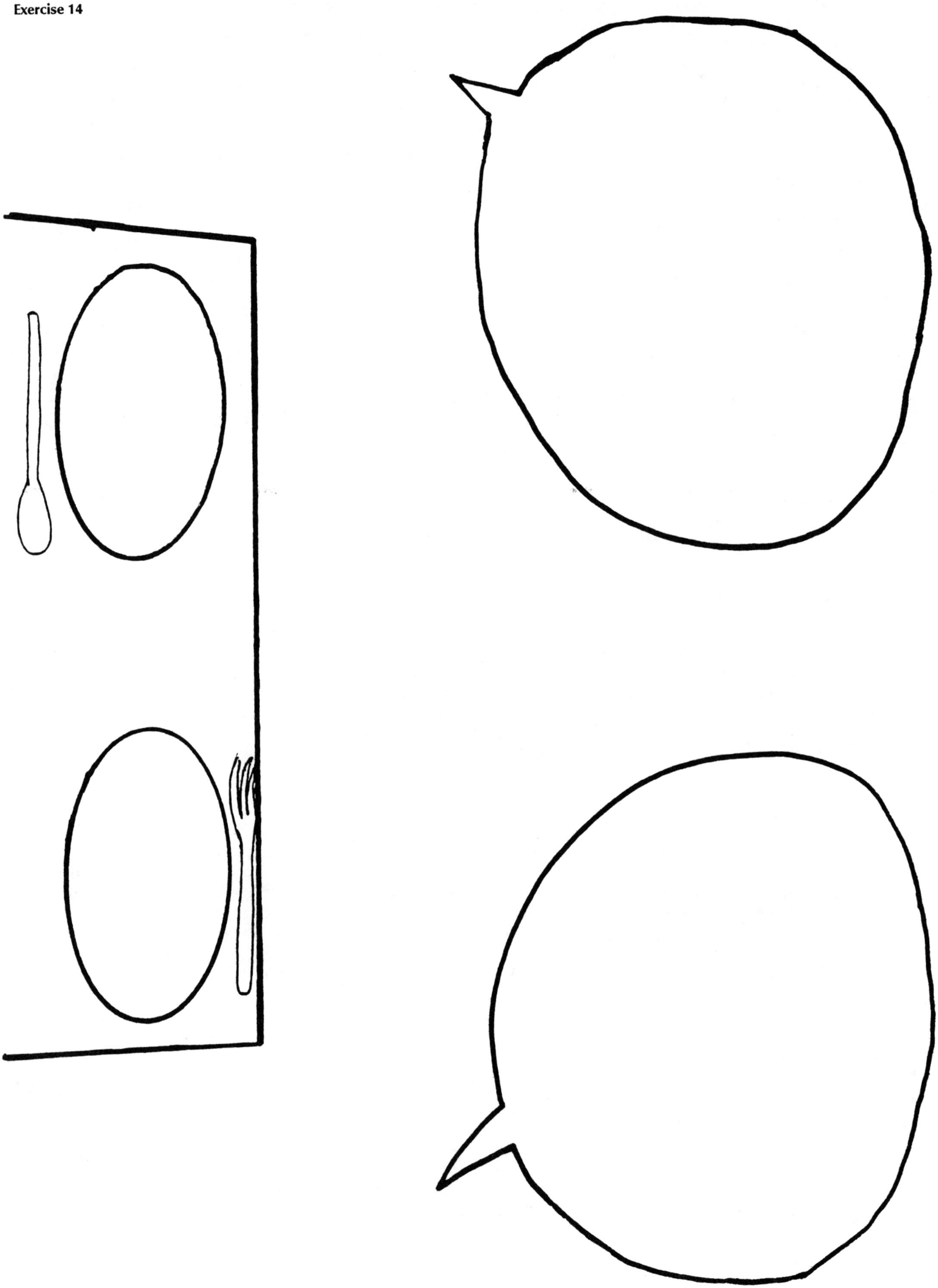

Exercise 15

INDIVIDUAL COLLAGE

Purpose:

    1. To compare self-image to other people's impressions of us.
    2. To facilitate group interaction by sharing personal information.

Materials:

    Magazines, scissors, glue, and blank paper.

Description:

    A. The leader describes a collage to the group as a collection of pictures which represent a common theme. The group is asked to give examples.
    B. While members are given the materials, they are told to think about the type of pictures that would tell something about themselves and their interests.
    C. Members are told to search for pictures that apply, cut them out, and glue them on the blank paper.

Group Discussion:

    Individual collages are passed around anonymously. Each member tries to guess what the collage reveals about the person who created it, and also guess who created it. Then, other group members give their opinion.

    The member who created it describes the significance of the picture in the collage. The group leader helps to highlight the personal qualities that each collage reveals.

    Often, this exercise leads members to reveal unknown interests and concerns. This leads to a better understanding of each member of the group.

    This exercise is effective for any group beyond the initial stage of development.

Exercise 16

THE GROUP TRUNK

Purpose:

1. To promote the dynamics involved in group task completion.
2. To develop insight through exploration of common needs.
3. To work towards a common goal in order to promote cohesion and group identity.

Materials:

Two copies of the illustration; crayons or markers.

Description:

A. A discussion is initiated on the differences between individual needs and group needs.
B. The group is divided into two teams. Each team chooses an illustrator.
C. While handing out materials, the leader asks both teams to think about what this group needs in order to continue to function and survive.
D. Team members discuss among themselves what is needed for the group. The illustrator then draws or writes in the empty trunk whatever is decided.

Group Discussion:

The group leader promotes discussion within each team. Then, when each illustration is completed, the teams discuss what is in their "trunk." The leader encourages them to suggest how each item in the trunk will help overcome the group's weaknesses. Common themes are focused on.

This exercise helps group members to better understand the needs of their group, and may motivate them to work together toward goals.

The group may choose to re-evaluate their needs by repeating this exercise several months later in order to explore how and if group needs have changed.

This exercise may be done with any group type, and works well in the early stages of group development to set general goals. In the later stages, it is effective in helping the group work through problems.

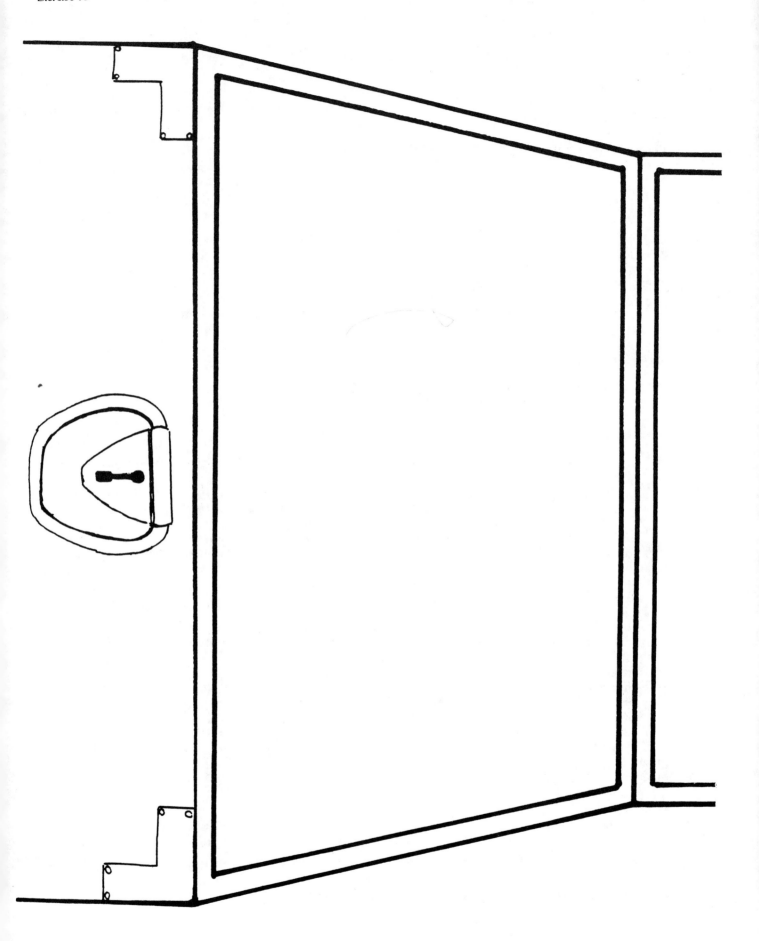

Exercise 17

FILL IN THE FACE

Purpose:

1. To provide an opportunity for self-disclosure.
2. To allow members to gain insight about themselves in a nonthreatening way.
3. To promote feedback about perceptions of self and others.

Materials:

One photocopy of the illustration for each member; pens, pencils, and crayons.

Description:

A. The leader prepares the group for this exercise by reading the incomplete word balloon on the illustration. The leader gives examples of how to complete it.
B. The group leader gives out materials, and asks members to complete the word balloon.
C. Members are told to complete the face in a way that best relates to the words.

Group Discussion:

Each group member shows his or her "face" and reads the completed cartoon balloon. The group is asked to comment on each face and word balloon.

The leader helps members to explore each other's feelings. Similarities and differences are compared. In some instances, members will reveal problems which the group may help to resolve.

Group members need to be able to think abstractly to complete this exercise. It is effective when used in the early stages of group development to facilitate self-disclosure.

Exercise 18

MAGAZINE COVER

Purpose:

1. To promote group cohesion by identifying topics of mutual concern and interest.
2. To share viewpoints through the free exchange of ideas.

Materials:

One photocopy of the illustration for each member; crayons or markers.

Description:

A. Members explore how an editor chooses a front page story.
B. While giving out the materials, the group leader tells members to think of a news-worthy story that would be of interest to many people.
C. Members are told to draw in the scene that would appear on the magazine cover.
D. When each drawing is completed, each member adds a related headline.

Discussion:

Each member describes his or her news story. Group members discuss how each story could influence their lives. In some groups, actual news stories will be presented and this will lead to a discussion of current events. In other groups, members will identify situations related to their personal concerns.

This exercise is effective with any group type at all stages of development because it may be interpreted on many levels.

Variation:

Each member re-creates an actual news story from the past which had tremendous impact on his or her life.

NATIONAL

80¢

SPECTATOR

LARGEST CIRCULATION OF ANY PAPER IN AMERICA

Exercise 19

GENIE WITH THREE WISHES

Purpose:

1. To share fantasies as an expression of one's needs.
2. To demonstrate universality through the recognition of common interests.

Materials:

One photocopy of the illustration for each member; crayons or markers.

Description:

A. The leader explores with the group the differences between wishes for oneself and wishes for others.
B. While giving out the materials, the leader tells the members to imagine a genie who will grant them three wishes.
C. Each member draws his or her wishes in the genie's puffs of smoke.

Group Discussion:

Participants discuss their wishes. The leader encourages members to ask each other how these wishes, if granted, would change their lives. Common themes are focused on. Group members discuss why they have wishes in common. Often, wishes address basic needs to be fulfilled, such as the need for money or clothing.

This exercise is effective with many group types at all stages of development.

Variation:

Members wish for personal qualities such as a sense of humor or more patience, rather than tangibles such as money or clothing.

THREE WISHES

Exercise 20

THE EMPTY ROOM

Purpose:

1. To achieve interpersonal learning; to see oneself as others do.
2. To focus on a common theme to reinforce group skills.
3. To respond to the needs and concerns of others.

Materials:

One photocopy of the illustration for each group member; pens, pencils, crayons, or markers.

Description:

A. The leader asks the group to describe various human needs.
B. The illustration of the empty room is given out to only one member of the group at a time.
C. That member is told to draw in one item which he or she thinks would make the member comfortable, relaxed, or happy in that room.
D. The illustration is then passed to the next person who adds an item to this room, which he or she thinks might make the original member happy.
E. The illustration is passed around the group until each member has added an item to the room for the original member.
F. This procedure is repeated until the group has created a room for every member.

Group Discussion:

Group leaders should remind participants to keep drawings small so that there will be room for every member of the group to add to the picture.

Members discuss what they are adding while they draw it. The whole group is asked to focus attention on one person's room at a time.

The leader encourages the group to ask questions as each item is added. While each member's room is being created, that member tells whether each item is important to him or her.

This exercise is effective with groups whose members have some familiarity with each other and are capable of insight into each other's needs.

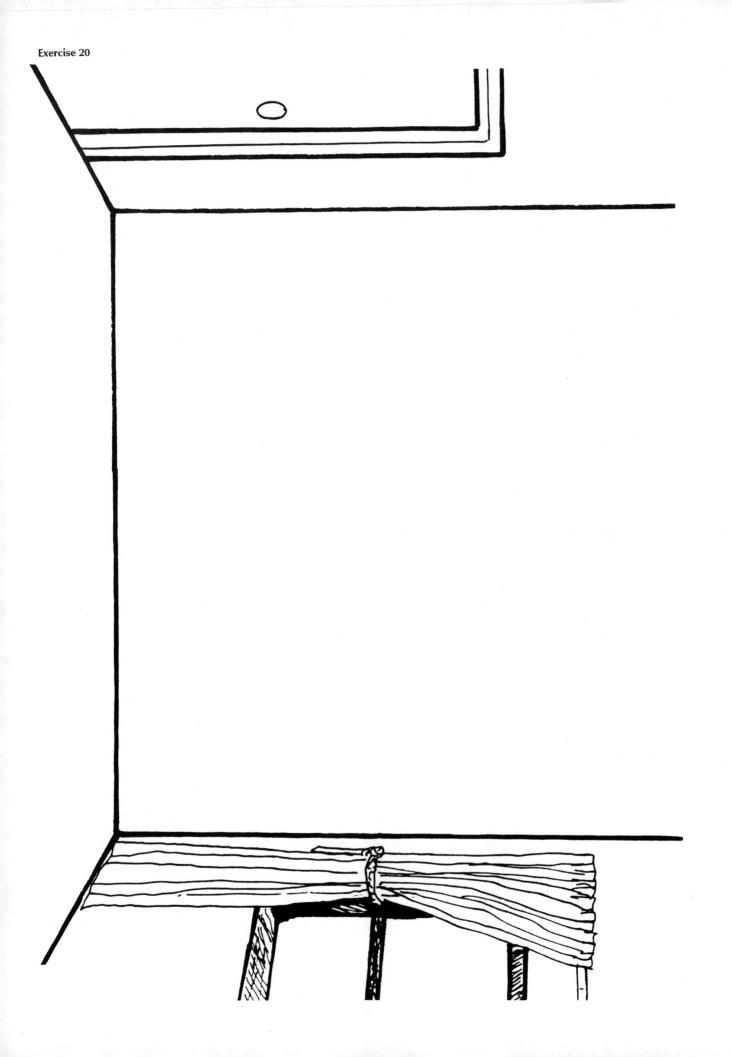

Exercise 21

CHANGING MYSELF

Purpose:

1. To promote self-improvement as a positive consequence of recognizing members' own weaknesses.
2. To incorporate group feedback into self-evaluation.
3. To recognize our potential in order to control more aspects of our lives.

Materials:

One photocopy of the illustration for each member; crayons, pens, and pencils.

Description:

A. Group discussion is directed toward the possibility of changing one's own personality.
B. While handing out the materials, the leader tells the members to imagine exchanging one aspect of their personalities for another.
C. In the circles provided, each member draws in the characteristic that is discarded, and the one that is acquired.
D. The sentences in the word balloons are completed to describe each drawing.

Group Discussion:

Each participant reads his or her completed word balloons, and shows the accompanying illustration. The leader encourages others to explore in more detail the reasons for each change. Related feelings are shared. Members focus on how they can help each other work toward the desired change.

Members generally demonstrate support and empathy for one another. This helps members feel better about themselves and recognize their own potential.

This exercise is designed for groups who are well-integrated, and are able to think abstractly.

Exercise 22

THE TELEPHONE CALL

Purpose:

1. To promote one-to-one interaction in a nonthreatening manner.
2. To experience the dynamics of shared task completion.

Materials:

One photocopy of the illustration for each member; yarn, magazines, scissors, paste, pens, and pencils.

Description:

A. The leader asks members to talk about the variety of possible conversations that people might have on the telephone.
B. The group is divided into pairs. The illustrations of a telephone are given out.
C. Each "telephone" is connected by string or yarn to the partner's phone.
D. Each pair looks through magazines together and chooses pictures of two people whom they imagine might be having a telephone conversation. They paste these chosen pictures onto their illustration.
E. Each pair decides what this conversation is about and writes a brief description of it on the telephone illustration.

Group Discussion:

Each pair reads their illustrations to the group. The leader encourages members to comment about whether these conversations could actually take place.

Each person is encouraged to suggest how the phone call would continue and end.

Members explore how they think these two callers feel about each other.

This exercise can be entertaining or revealing, depending upon the composition of the group. It is most useful during the early stages of group development because it is nonthreatening.

Exercise 23

PHOTO ALBUM

Purpose:

1. To develop a climate for group interaction through self-disclosure of personal information.
2. To share memories and compare experiences.
3. To increase understanding and acceptance of others.

Materials:

One photocopy of the illustration for each member; crayons and markers.

Description:

A. The leader asks members to describe the significance of photographs in people's lives.
B. Each member is given the illustration simulating a photo album page.
C. Group members read the photo captions together.
D. The leader asks group members to illustrate each of the four photos.

Group Discussion:

Each member discusses his or her "photos" with the group, and reveals related feelings. The leader encourages questions, and notes similarities and differences in choices.

The leader asks members to expand on the importance of these photos in their lives. Some groups may wish to staple pages together to make an album. The discussion may evolve into a reminiscence session.

This exercise is effective with a wide variety of groups, and is most useful during the early stages of development, because it is nonthreatening.

PHOTOS BY _____

My Favorite Animal

My Favorite Place

A Nice Person

A Special Belonging

Exercise 24

DOUBLE EXPOSURE

Purpose:

1. To follow directions and complete tasks.
2. To promote interaction by sharing viewpoints.

Materials:

Each color chart and each illustration should be photocopied for half the number of people in the group (see description); crayons.

Description:

A. Two illustrations and two color charts are used in this activity.
B. Divide the room into two teams. All members of each team get the same illustration.
C. Half of each team gets the color-by-number chart. The other half gets the color-by-letter chart.
D. Members are instructed to color illustrations according to the code of their color chart.

Group Discussion:

The group's discussion first centers on the variety of pictures created. Members are then encouraged to verbalize different interpretations of the various pictures.

Members are asked to tell how they think the people in each picture feel about their situation.

One possible outcome of this exercise is that group members can create stories about the pictures they have illustrated. This may be done individually or in teams.

This exercise is effective with any group type, and may be used during all stages of group development.

COLOR BY LETTER CHART*

(people using this chart ignore all numbers)

Y = Yellow
W = White
U = Blue
B = Brown
K = Black
R = Red
P = Pink
G = Green
N = Orange

COLOR BY NUMBER CHART*

(people using this chart ignore all letters)

1 = Yellow
2 = White
3 = Blue
4 = Brown
5 = Black
6 = Red
7 = Pink
8 = Green
9 = Orange

*For Exercise 24

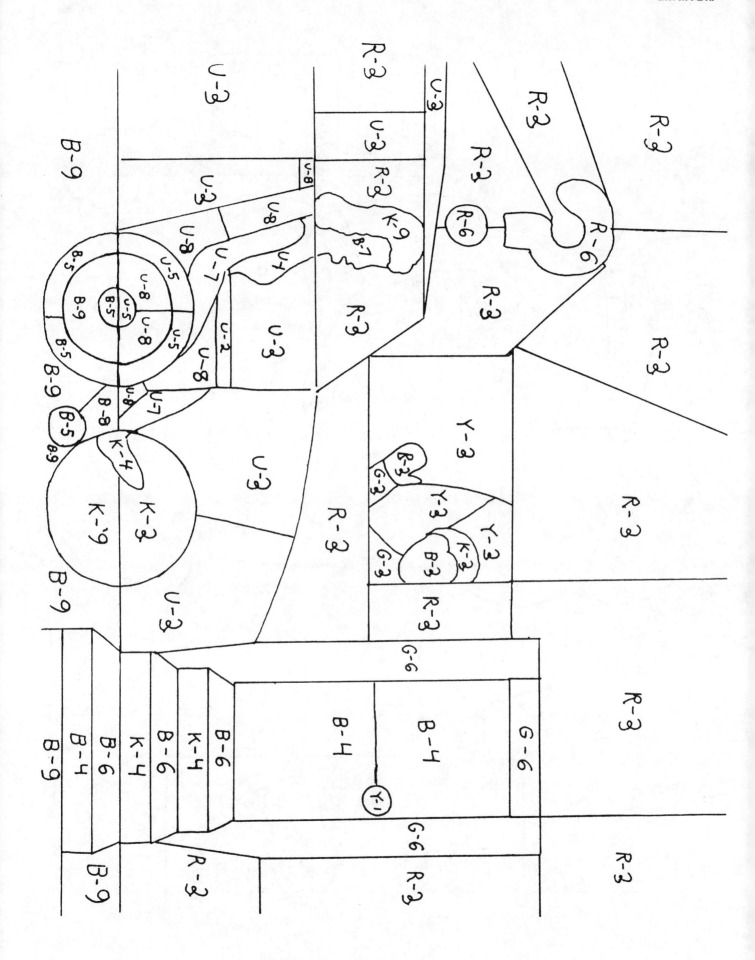

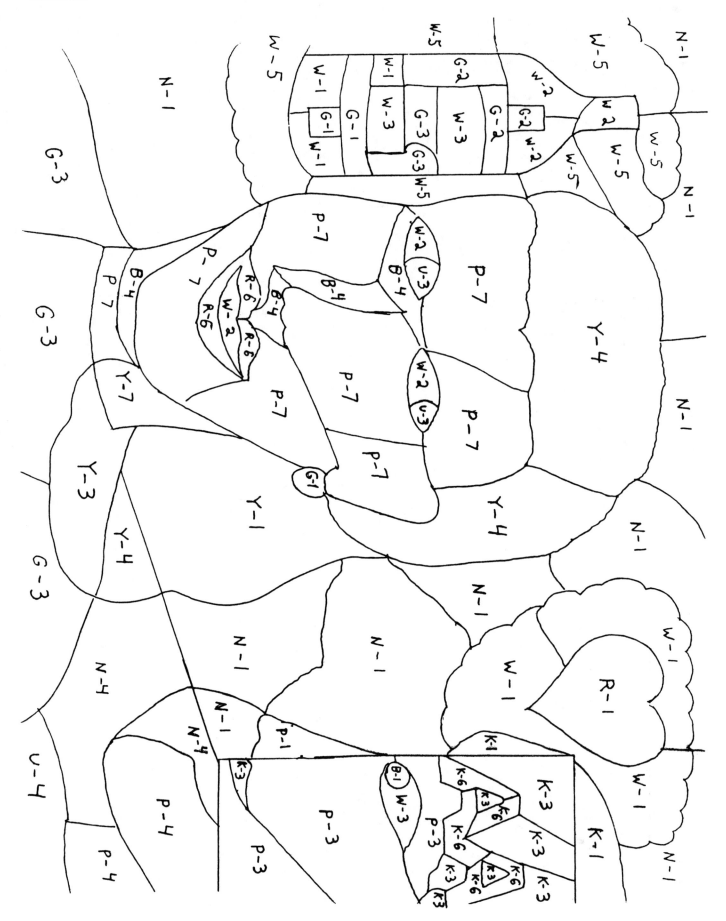

Exercise 25

THE BLANK CHECK

Purpose:

1. To provide an opportunity for open communication in order to identify topics of concern.
2. To recognize and understand each other's needs.
3. To promote group identity and cohesion by bonding together and being supportive of one another.

Materials:

One photocopy of the illustration for each group member; crayons or markers.

Description:

A. The leader holds up the picture of a blank check and asks how it might relate to a common fantasy.
B. Each participant is given the illustration of the blank check.
C. Group members fill in their own names (pay to _____), an emotional need (for feeling _____), and the dollar amount they would spend to resolve this need.
D. The papers are collected, and then re-distributed so that each member gets someone else's check.
E. Upon reading the check received, members draw in a practical suggestion of how they would fill that person's emotional need.
F. The completed check is returned to the member whose name is on it.

Group Discussion:

Members identify topics of concern by revealing to the entire group the personal need addressed on the check. The group leader encourages other members to explore the importance of each member's need. In addition, the members discuss whether they can help meet each other's needs *as a group.*

The idea of a check often leads members to think of material needs. The group leader reminds members to think about emotional needs. This exercise can be done with a variety of groups beyond the early stage of development.

Variation:

The leader puts each member's name on a separate blank check. These are distributed at random. Each member thinks of an item needed by that person, draws it in, and writes an amount on the check.

708- B76 - 00871-22   NO. 555

DATE _____ 19 ___

PAY TO _____ $ [.   ]

AMOUNT_____

★★★★ —— THE UNITED
▬US.▬ STATES BANK

FOR FEELING _____   SIGNATURE _____

Exercise 26

OPEN THE DOOR

Purpose:

1. To promote heightened awareness of self and others by sharing fantasies.
2. To explore what personal expectations reveal about oneself.
3. To develop group cohesion through mutual self-disclosure.

Materials:

One photocopy of the illustration for each member, folded in half at the door hinge like a greeting card; pens, pencils, and crayons.

Description:

A. The leader holds up the folded illustration and asks the members to tell what they think will be asked of them.
B. While handing out the materials, the leader tells the group members to imagine what they could expect to find behind a closed door.
C. Members illustrate their expectations on the inside of the folded page.

Group Discussion:

Each member presents what he or she drew, and describes why it was chosen as a drawing. The leader asks members to explore what these expectations represent. The group discusses what this tells about each member. The leader encourages members to be supportive of each other when unpleasant expectations are revealed.

The responses to this exercise are varied and unpredictable, often revealing something new about each member.

This exercise can be used with any group type and, because it can be interpreted on many levels, it is effective during all stages of group development.

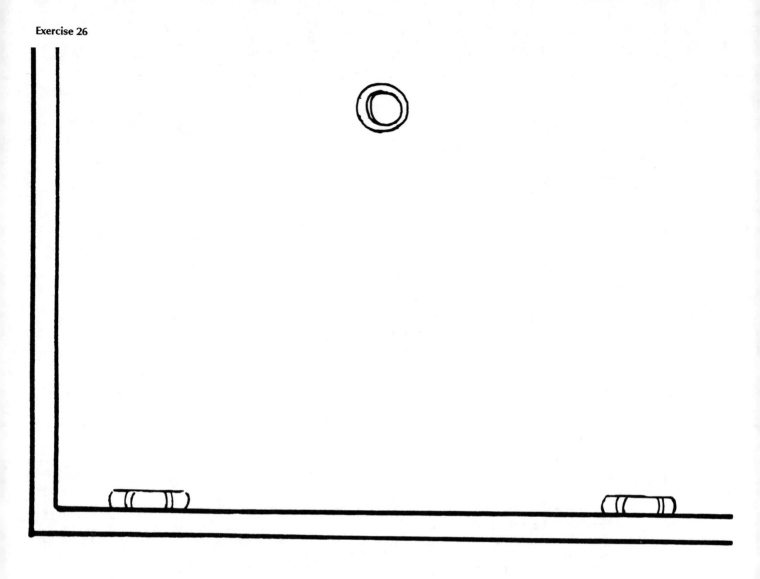

Exercise 27

HAND HOLDING HAND

Purpose:

1. To encourage self-disclosure and one-on-one interaction in a nonthreatening manner.
2. To promote trust through risk-taking.
3. To increase understanding and acceptance of others.

Materials:

One photocopy of the illustration for each member; crayons or markers.

Description:

A. The leader initiates a discussion about how a group can create an atmosphere in which two group members can be made comfortable about talking to each other in front of the rest of the group.
B. The names of group members are put into a "hat." Each member draws a name out of the hat.
C. Group members are then given the illustration "Hand Holding Hand," and told to draw themselves and a picture of the person whose name they have picked out of the hat.

Group Discussion:

Each member asks the person he or she has chosen to reveal something about himself or herself. The member then reveals a personal thing to that person. The leader encourages them to ask more about what is revealed.

Each dialogue takes place in front of the group. The group comments about what was learned from each dialogue.

As dialogues follow one another, the group climate often becomes safer, and remaining members are more willing to take the risk of self-disclosure. This exercise works best with groups that are more insightful and in the later stages of group development.

Exercise 28

GROUP COLLAGE

Purpose:

1. To reinforce group skills in task performance and decision making.
2. To reflect on a group experience in order to better understand its dynamics.

Materials:

Scissors, magazines, large oak tag paper, and paste or glue.

Description:

A. The leader tells group members they are going to be working on a collage. This collage will be a collection of magazine pictures which represent a specific theme.
B. The group members are asked to choose a theme. Some examples might be love, food, nature, family, or sports.
C. They are given magazines and asked to cut out pictures representing the themes.
D. Members decide, as a group, how to arrange these pictures.

Group Discussion:

The leader asks the members to describe why a particular theme was chosen, and together they discuss why certain illustrations were picked. The leader helps the group reflect on its own dynamics. They explore who emerged as a leader(s) of this exercise, whether there was a balance of input from other members, and how they felt about working on a group project.

Exploration of the group dynamics is the most important consequence of this exercise. A variety of groups at all stages of development should find this exercise effective.

Variation:

Divide members into teams to work on chosen themes.

Exercise 29

WORDS FOR FACT OR FANTASY

Purpose:

1. To provide an opportunity for communication in a nonthreatening way.
2. To share responsibility in order to complete a task.

Materials:

One photocopy of the illustration for each member; crayons, pens, or pencils.

Description:

A. A brief discussion is initiated about how a word can have different meanings to different people. The group gives examples.
B. Each member is given the illustration and told to write down any word that has a special meaning to him or her. The leader collects, shuffles, and re-distributes the papers.
C. Each member draws a picture corresponding to the word written on the page.
D. Papers are then reshuffled and re-distributed. Each member writes a brief story about the word and illustration received. This story can be based either on fact or fantasy.

Group Discussion:

Members, in turn, describe the word and picture they have received. They then read the accompanying story.

Members comment on whether they believe the story being told is true or false.

Group members explore their feelings about performing a task that is dependent on previous stages being completed by others.

This exercise is best suited for members who have some ability to think abstractly. It is effective at all stages of group development.

FACT OR FANTASY?

① WORD _____

② PICTURE

③ STORY

Exercise 30

FACE TO FACE

Purpose:

1. To identify how facial expressions represent the way people feel.
2. To recognize the causes and appropriateness of moods and emotions.

Materials:

One photocopy of the illustration for each member; crayons or markers.

Description:

A. An initial discussion focuses on how facial expressions reveal feelings. Members demonstrate with expressions.
B. Each participant is given the illustration and told to complete the face to show the mood and feeling of the person.
C. On the back of the paper, each participant draws or writes the experience which possibly resulted in that emotion.

Group Discussion:

The group looks at each participant's drawing. They all guess the mood that each face represents, and tell why it represents that mood. The leader encourages members to reveal their true feelings about the face they drew.

The discussion expands on the written event that led to the mood. Group members discuss whether they feel this is an appropriate feeling, considering the event depicted.

Often, members project what they are feeling at the moment. Through this exercise, they are able to share this in a nonthreatening way.

This exercise is effective with groups who have some insight and the ability to think abstractly. It is useful in all stages of group development.

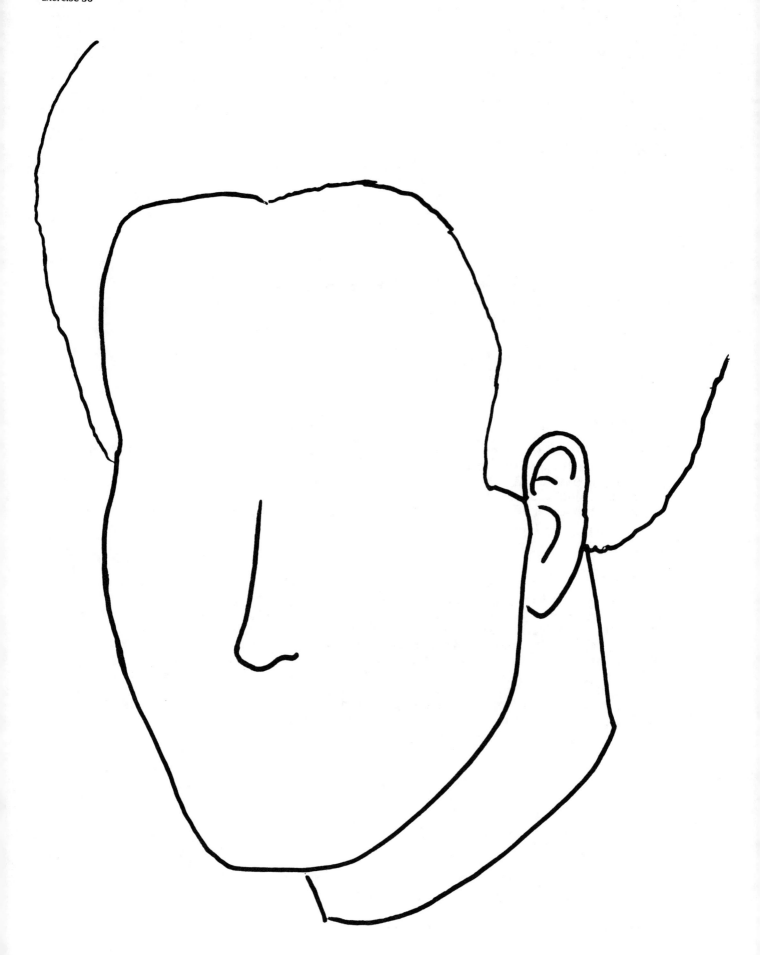

Exercise 31

THE DRAWER

Purpose:

1. To reveal oneself through choice of significant objects.
2. To recognize the needs of others.

Materials:

One photocopy of the illustration for each member; crayons or markers.

Description:

A. The leader begins this exercise by asking members to discuss why certain objects have sentimental value.
B. While handing out materials, the leader tells the group members to think about their important or treasured possessions.
C. The members illustrate these possessions in the open drawer.

Group Discussion:

Each member presents his or her drawing, describes the chosen possessions, and tells why they are of special importance. The leader encourages members to add to each other's drawer and to explain the possible significance of that possession.

Often, the discussion evolves further because the chosen possessions relate to immediate needs or special memories.

Because of the open-ended format of this exercise, it is effective with a variety of groups during all stages of group development.

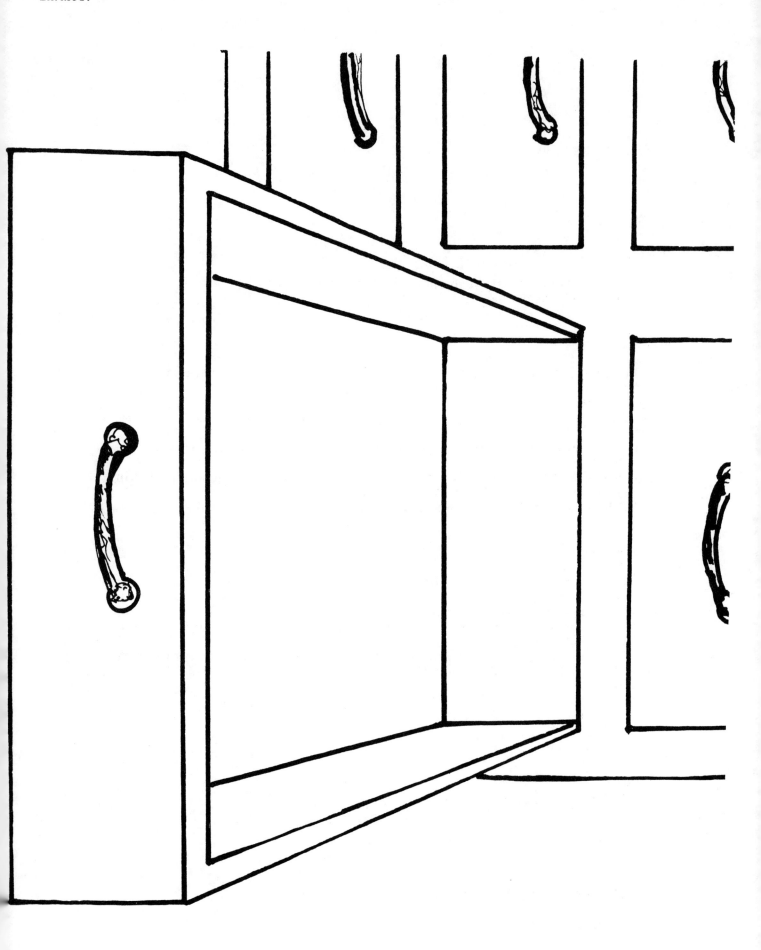

Exercise 32

THE CHECKOUT LINE

Purpose:

1. To recognize each other's needs.
2. To promote money management skills.
3. To advance the acceptance of group feedback regarding individual decision-making skills.

Materials:

One photocopy of the illustration for each member; crayons or markers.

Description:

A. The leader prepares the group by asking them to discuss the prices of things today compared with the cost of things in the past.
B. While handing out the materials, the leader asks group members to think about what they would buy on a shopping spree.
C. The group decides on an amount of money to be spent by each member.
D. Participants draw in a realistic purchase with the amount of money they were assigned.

Group Discussion:

Each member presents what he or she purchased to the rest of the group. Members are helped to recognize what these purchases reveal about their needs. In addition, the leader asks the group if the chosen purchases were realistic, given the amount of money which each had to spend. The feedback given may lead to a better understanding of how to budget money.

This exercise is effective with a variety of group types at any stage of development.

Variation:

Members draw what could be purchased as a gift for someone special. Discussion focuses on how members determine the needs of others, and whether these purchases are realistic, given the amount of money they have to spend.

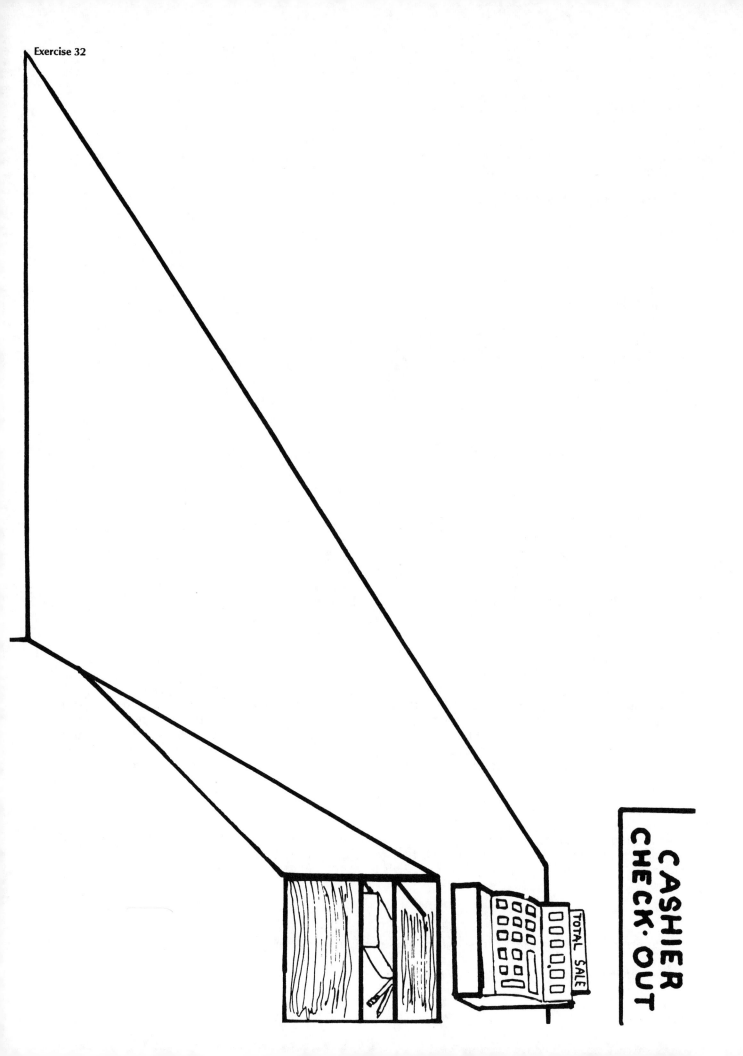

Exercise 32

CASHIER
CHECK·OUT

TOTAL SALE
000.00

Exercise 33

WHAT'S FOUND IN A COMMUNITY ROOM

Purpose:

1. To facilitate a recognition of a common bond among group members.
2. To practice goal-setting and task completion.

Materials:

One photocopy of the illustration for each member; scotch tape, crayons or markers.

Description:

A. The group discusses what rooms they all share in common. Then they choose one of these rooms to use in this exercise.
B. While handing out materials, the leader tells members to describe some of the experiences they have had in the shared room.
C. Each person draws the chosen experience on the illustration.
D. When completed, these sheets are taped together forming one long illustration of a community room.

Group Discussion:

Starting at one end of the illustrated room, the leader asks each group member to describe the experience that he or she drew. The leader encourages feedback when each is presented, and helps members recognize any similarities between them.

It is important to discuss feelings which members have about the chosen experiences to facilitate a recognition of common bonds that they share.

This exercise helps members to express many types of experiences with varied moods and feelings. It is most applicable with residents or inpatients since they share many rooms in common.

Exercise 33

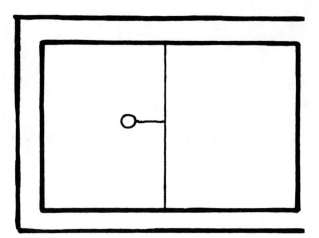

Exercise 34

THE DREAM

Purpose:

1. To explore each individual's significant concerns.
2. To share fantasies in order to provide heightened awareness of self and others.
3. To identify common fears.

Materials:

One photocopy of the illustration for each member; markers or crayons.

Description:

A. The leader shows the illustration and instructs members to guess what will be asked.
B. While handing out the materials, the leader tells the members to think about a dream, either real or imagined, that enters their mind.
C. Each member draws scenes from the dream on his or her illustration.

Group Discussion:

Members describe their illustration to the group, and disclose its significance to them. It is important that they describe the mood of the dream as well. The leader encourages group members to discuss what they think this reveals about each person.

Although content of dreams will vary, members will be encouraged to recognize common underlying fears and concerns. A frequent outcome is that members choose to share actual dreams.

This exercise can be interpreted on many levels. It is useful with a wide variety of groups in all stages of development.

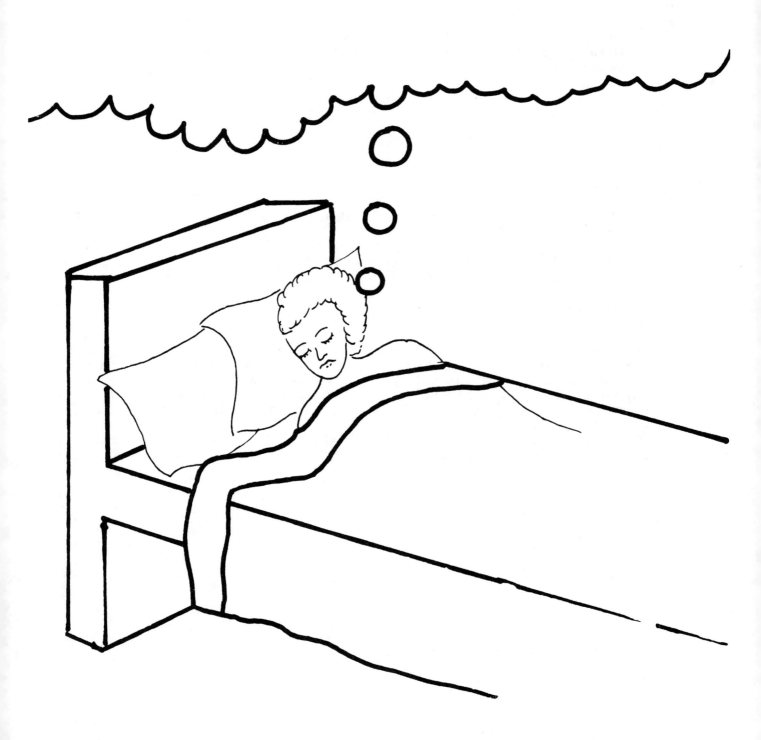

Exercise 35

THE BUDDY SYSTEM

Purpose:

1. To encourage self-disclosure through one-on-one interaction.
2. To follow directions and share task completion.
3. To increase understanding and acceptance of others.

Materials:

One photocopy of the illustration for each member; pens or pencils and crayons.

Description:

A. Members are asked to share their feelings about getting to know one another better.
B. Participants are paired off and told to draw themselves and their partners in the appropriate areas of the illustration provided.
C. Participants are told to ask each other how they feel today.
D. Participants are asked to describe not only their own, but their partner's feelings in the spaces provided.

Group Discussion:

Each pair describes what they found out about each other. Then they are asked to share their drawings, and tell why they attributed certain feelings to each other. The leader encourages the other members to comment on the accuracy of the feelings described. Any feelings of anxiety evoked among members should be explored.

This exercise was designed for groups that have by now established some degree of trust, and which are in the later stages of group development.

MY NAME

TODAY I FEEL

PARTNER

TODAY I FEEL

Exercise 36

THE DINNER PLATE

Purpose:

1. To accept group feedback; to use it constructively.
2. To understand the need for good nutrition.

Materials:

One photocopy of the illustration for each member; markers or crayons.

Description:

A. While handing out the materials, the group leader engages the members in a brief discussion about the importance of good nutrition.
B. Each member draws a picture of what he or she would consider to be a nutritionally balanced meal.

Group Discussion:

Members present their meals, and describe what they feel is the nutritional value. Others discuss whether they think the meals are balanced. The leader encourages members to talk about favorite snacks that are also nutritious.

In some instances, depending upon the setting or group, the discussion of nutrition or diet may be pursued at other times. A dietitian or reference materials may be included in such a follow-up.

Because this exercise is informative rather than introspective, it works well with a variety of groups in all stages of development.

Variation:

The group members draw a meal for a diabetic, or for someone on a weight-loss (weight-gain) diet.

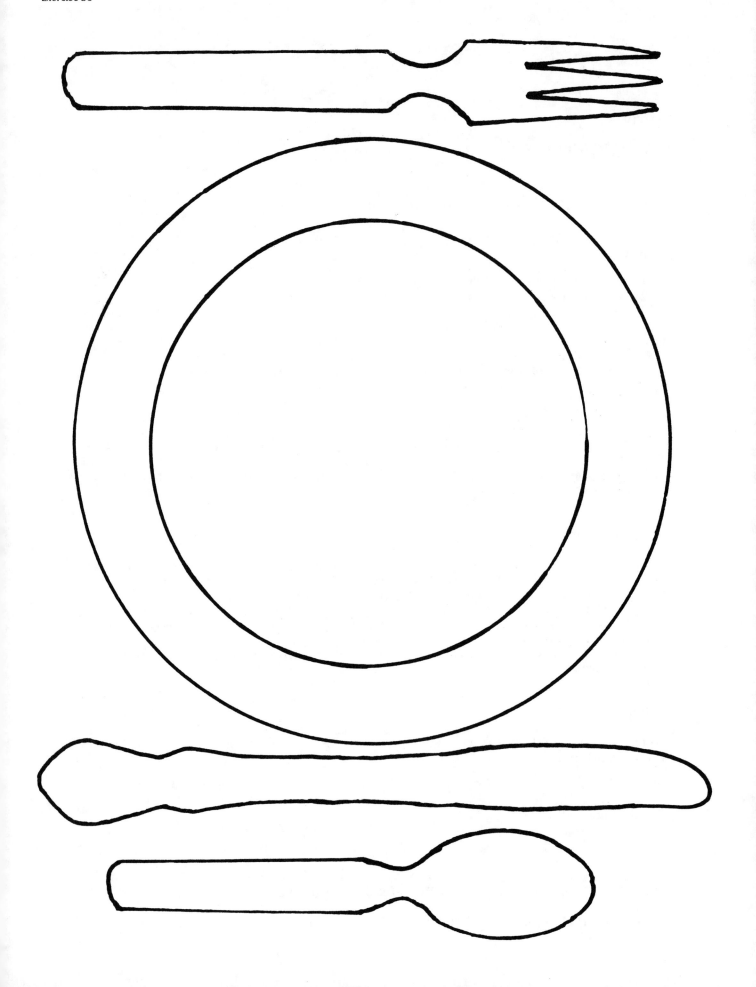

Exercise 37

THE CHAIN LETTER

Purpose:

1. To focus on a common theme in order to reinforce group skills.
2. To share responsibility in order to complete a task.
3. To reflect on a group experience in order to better understand its dynamics.

Materials:

Two photocopies of the illustration; additional blank paper; pens or pencils.

Description:

A. The leader prepares the group for this exercise by asking members to discuss how they feel about working together on a group project. They discuss the process of sharing creatively.
B. The group is divided into two teams, and told to choose captains.
C. Each team is given the illustration of the "chain letter" and blank paper.
D. The group leader or team captain provides the first sentence of the open-ended story. Here are two sample sentences to begin each story:

   (1) It was a very hot day in the....
   (2) Everyone in the group was very quiet that day. Suddenly....

E. Then, each team member takes a turn and adds to the story as it develops.

Group Discussion:

Team captains read the stories to the rest of the group. Group members are encouraged to talk about how they arrived at a common theme, and possibly how the theme changed as the story progressed. The leader helps members to explore whether this shared task was easier or more difficult than individual projects.

One possible outcome of this exercise: Members may reveal and add personal information to the conception of the story as it develops. The group's dynamics, and members' roles may become more apparent to the leader.

This exercise is effective with groups that may need help with development of interpersonal skills.

Exercise 38

THE DOORBELL

Purpose:

    1. To reveal feelings.
    2. To identify the qualities that attract people to others.

Materials:

    One photocopy of the illustration for group members; markers or crayons.

Description:

    A. The group leader encourages members to describe some of the positive qualities of the people they like.
    B. The materials are handed out, and members look at the illustration. The leader asks the group to think about who they would most like to have ring their door-bell.
    C. Each member draws in the person he or she would most like to see when the door opens.

Group Discussion:

    Members reveal who is on the other side of their door. They describe the qualities they like about that person. The leader encourages questions from the group about the person drawn and his or her relationship to that member. The leader asks the group to interpret what each drawing reveals about each member's needs. Concentration can be on common themes.
    Members sometimes choose to illustrate each other behind the door. They focus on the positive qualities of fellow members. This exercise can be interpreted on many levels, therefore, it is effective with a variety of groups at all stages of development.

Variation:

    Each member draws the person whom he or she would least like to see at the open door.

Exercise 38

Exercise 39

WORDS OF WISDOM AND COMFORT

Purpose:

1. To encourage interpersonal learning through the sharing of constructive responses to negative experiences.
2. To promote insight and empathy.
3. To reassure members that they can help each other.

Materials:

One photocopy of the illustration for each group member; pens, pencils, and crayons.

Description:

A. The group leader initiates a discussion of what it means to be supportive and reassuring. Members are encouraged to give specific examples of how to do this.
B. Members are given the accompanying illustration. They are told to draw in a picture of who they think might be making the comments in the word balloons.
C. Each member completes the reassuring remarks at the bottom of the page.

Group Discussion:

Individual members share their drawings and read their comments. Members are asked to reveal whether they can identify with the given statements. Each member explains why he or she gave a particular response. Often, members will personalize this exercise more than expected.

This exercise is designed for groups whose members are insightful and capable of abstract reasoning.

I'VE GOT NO REAL HOME

DON'T WORRY BECAUSE...

NOBODY LIKES ME

WE ALL FEEL THAT WAY AT TIMES, HOWEVER...

IT MAKES ME UPSET TO BE SO FORGETFUL

IT IS UPSETTING BUT YOU'RE VERY GOOD...

Exercise 40

EYE OF THE BEHOLDER

Purpose:

1. To promote group cohesiveness and interaction by exploring the interests of individual members.
2. To concentrate on details in order to complete a task.
3. To compare different interpretations and perspectives in order to learn about each other.

Materials:

An ample supply of illustrations for the expected rounds; crayons or markers.

Description:

A. The leader begins this exercise by introducing the theme of the importance of listening to each other. Members are asked to share their feelings about *not* being listened to.
B. While handing out the materials, the leader asks members to think of someone or something such as a parent, a friend, their homes, a scene from a movie, or an incident in their lives.
C. In each round of this exercise, one person describes what he or she is thinking, while the rest of the group illustrates their perception of it.

Group Discussion:

Separate discussions follow each round. Drawings are visually and verbally compared.

The leader asks presenting members if they thought they were listened to by the group, and how they felt about it. Group members look for similarities and differences in their interpretations of what was described.

In a task this structured, most members will listen to each other, but their interpretations will vary. Though this exercise is primarily designed to help members get acquainted with each other in a newly formed group, it can be used at any stage of development in a variety of groups.

Exercise 41

WHAT COMES NEXT?

Purpose:

1. To understand the relationships between cause and effect.
2. To develop a climate for group interaction by sharing individual perceptions.

Materials:

Assorted pre-cut magazine pictures to fit the description below; blank paper, paste, crayons or markers.

Description:

A. The leader describes open-ended situations and asks for examples of what action might be expected to follow. For example, if the leader were to describe two people holding hands, some members might say a kiss will follow.
B. Each member is given a picture from a magazine in which some action could follow. That picture is pasted on the left half of the page.
C. On the right half, the group is asked to illustrate what action they think will come next.
D. When the task is completed, the paper is folded so that only the magazine picture is face up.

Group Discussion:

One member at a time holds up his or her folded exercise, revealing only the side with the magazine picture. The leader draws the other members into a discussion of what the picture represents, and what action may follow. The leader then asks the presenting member to disclose the follow-up event illustrated on the paper. The group is encouraged to explore what feelings may be related to the expected outcome.

This exercise may be entertaining or revealing depending on the composition of the group. It is effective at any stage of group development.

Exercise 42

THE MAN AND THE WOMAN

Purpose:

1. To explore sex role stereotypes in order to increase awareness of our own attitudes.
2. To incorporate group feedback into self-evaluation.

Materials:

Blank paper, assorted magazines, scissors, paper clips; one photocopy of the illustration for each member.

Description:

A. The group leader asks the members what is meant by sex role stereotyping. Examples are given by members. The leader also asks the members if they think there are actual differences between the sexes.
B. Each participant is given the illustration along with magazines. Members are told to cut out items which they think specifically pertain to males or females. They attach these pictures with a paper clip to the illustrations they believe to be appropriate.

Group Discussion:

As members show each chosen picture, the leader encourages spontaneous feedback from the group. Members look for similarities and differences in choices as the discussion progresses.

This exercise may lead to the demonstration of a wide variety of beliefs, and the discussion may be continued at other times.

Because of the controversial subject matter, this exercise is recommended for groups that have already established a degree of trust between members.

Exercise 43

WISHING WELL

Purpose:

    1. To identify and interpret individual and group needs.
    2. To promote recognition of common bonds among group members.

Materials:

One photocopy of the illustration for each member; crayons or markers.

Description:

    A. The leader encourages members to reveal some of their individual needs to each other. The needs of the group are also discussed.
    B. The leader distributes the materials.
    C. Each member draws wishes, "for me," "for someone else in the group," and "for the group as a whole" into the corresponding areas of the illustration.

Group Discussion:

Individual members disclose the wish "for me," and the reason for it. The group leader encourages members to say what they think this reveals about each person.

Next, the leader focuses on the wish "for someone else in the group," and asks that person to reply.

Then, everyone is asked to respond to the wish "for the group as a whole." After all illustrations have been shared, similar wishes are identified and the group leader emphasizes the common bond between members.

Since wishes for each group member are involved, this exercise should be used with groups whose members are well-acquainted with each other.

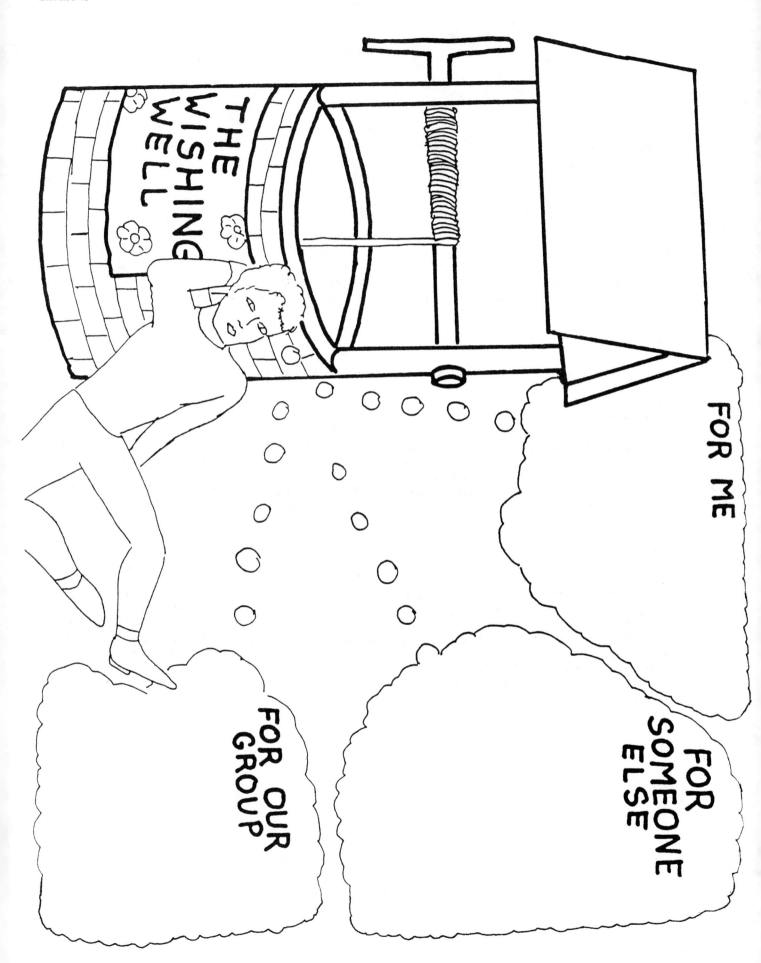

Exercise 44

SURPRISE!

Purpose:

1. To share fantasies in order to heighten awareness of self and others.
2. To explore how individual expectations represent needs.
3. To develop group cohesion through mutual self-disclosure.

Materials:

One photocopy of the illustration for each member; crayons or markers.

Description:

A. The leader engages the group in a brief discussion about distinguishing between a surprise and an expected event.
B. Each participant is given the illustration. Members draw a situation or an event which they think will surprise them when entering the room.
C. The leader encourages members to be specific about where this room is located.

Group Discussion:

Members discuss their illustrations, and describe their feelings. The leader should ask whether these situations or events had really happened to them in the past.

The group discusses what these expectations represent and reveal about each member. The leader helps members explore what they would do or feel in similar situations. The leader encourages members to be supportive when a disagreeable expectation is revealed.

Responses to this exercise are varied and unpredictable, often revealing something new about each member.

This exercise can be used with a variety of groups at all stages of development because it can be interpreted on many levels.

Exercise 44

Exercise 45

THE RAILROAD TRACK

Purpose:

1. To share memories in order to enhance self-disclosure.
2. To compare life experiences in order to learn more about each other.
3. To share feedback in a nonthreatening way.

Materials:

Tape, crayons or markers; enough photocopies of the two illustrations so that equal numbers of each illustration are distributed.

Description:

A. The leader shows both illustrations to the group. Members are asked to tell what each illustration looks like, and what they think this exercise might be about.
B. Half of the group members are given one illustration of the railroad track. The remaining half of the group are given the other illustration of the track. Then all members are told to draw a favorite place they have lived in or visited.
C. When they have completed the illustrations, the group leader tapes the illustrations together, joining all tracks. Display the resulting railroad line so that all the members can see it.

Group Discussion:

An imaginary train stops at all the stations so that members can describe their drawings. The leader asks members to expand on the importance of their chosen place, and share any significant events that took place there. Related feelings are explored. The group leader asks the other members if they would be interested in visiting the places described.

This discussion often evolves into a reminiscence discussion. It is effective with a variety of groups, and is useful with groups in the early stages of development as it relies on a nonthreatening form of self-disclosure.

Variation:

The members illustrate places they would like to visit *as a group*. The group discusses the significance of each chosen place, and describes what the group would do at each destination.

Exercise 45a

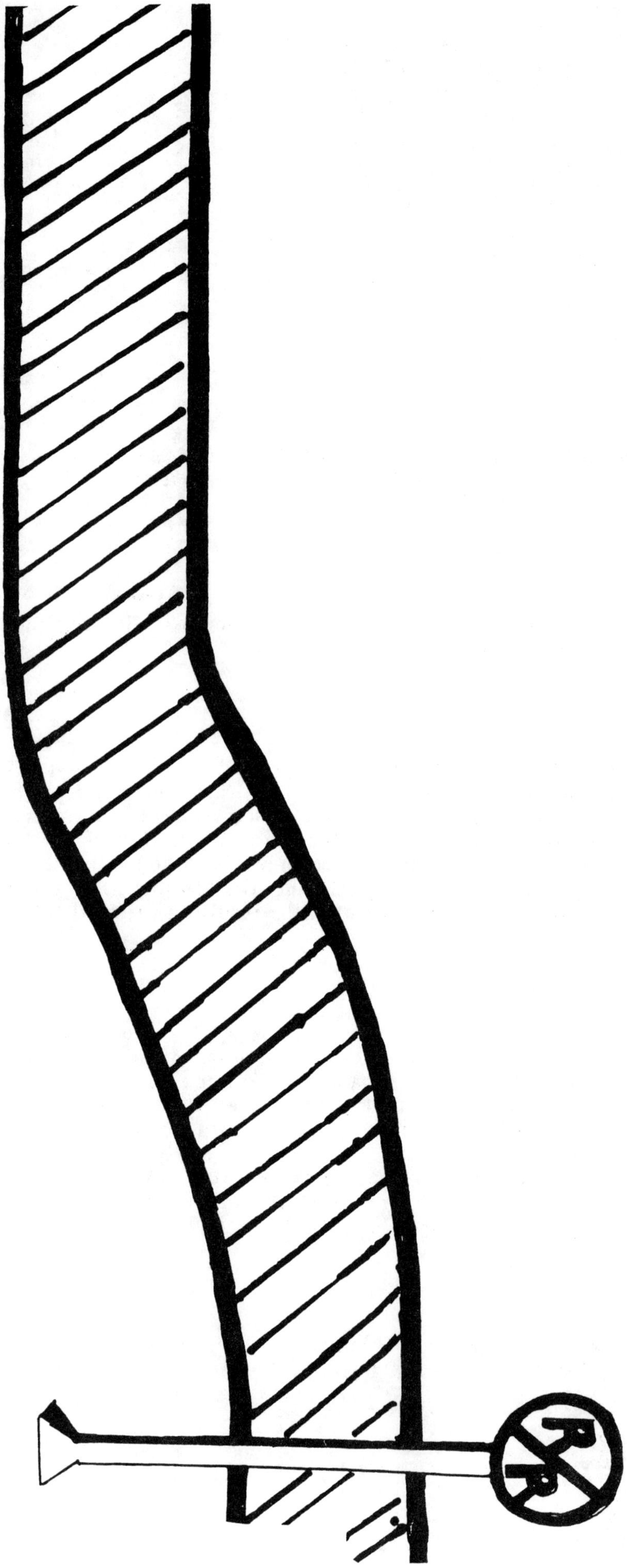

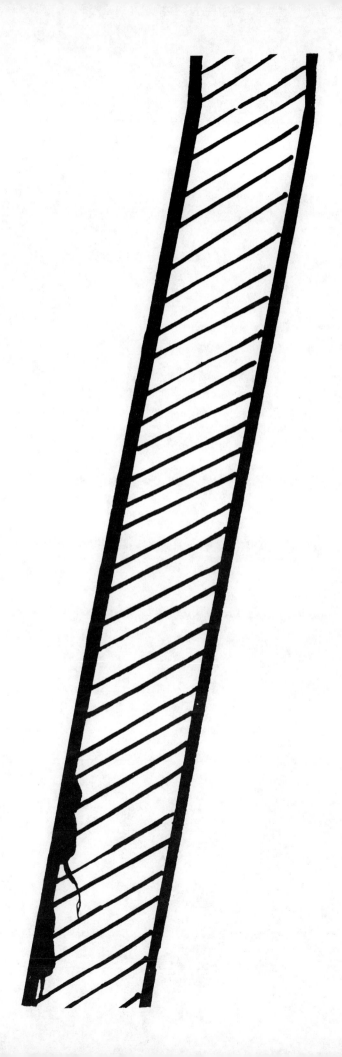

Exercise 46

SHOPPER'S SWEEPSTAKES

Purpose:

1. To reveal self through choice of objects.
2. To explore the needs of others through the expression of their wishes and desires.

Materials:

One photocopy of the illustration for group members; markers or crayons.

Description:

A. The leader engages the group in a discussion revolving around the fantasy of being given things free of charge from a store.
B. The illustration is passed out and each member is told to pretend that he or she has won a free 20 minute shopping spree in a store.
C. They illustrate the items that they choose to take for themselves on this shopping spree.

Group Discussion:

Each participant describes the contents of his or her shopping cart and explains the significance of each item taken. The leader encourages members to say what they think this reveals about each person.

Members are asked to add items to each other's cart and give their reasons. The items chosen will often address basic needs.

This exercise is nonthreatening, and can be interpreted on many levels. Therefore, it is effective with a variety of groups.

Variation:

Members choose each other's name at random and shop for items which they think the other person would appreciate. The discussion focuses on understanding the perceived needs of others.

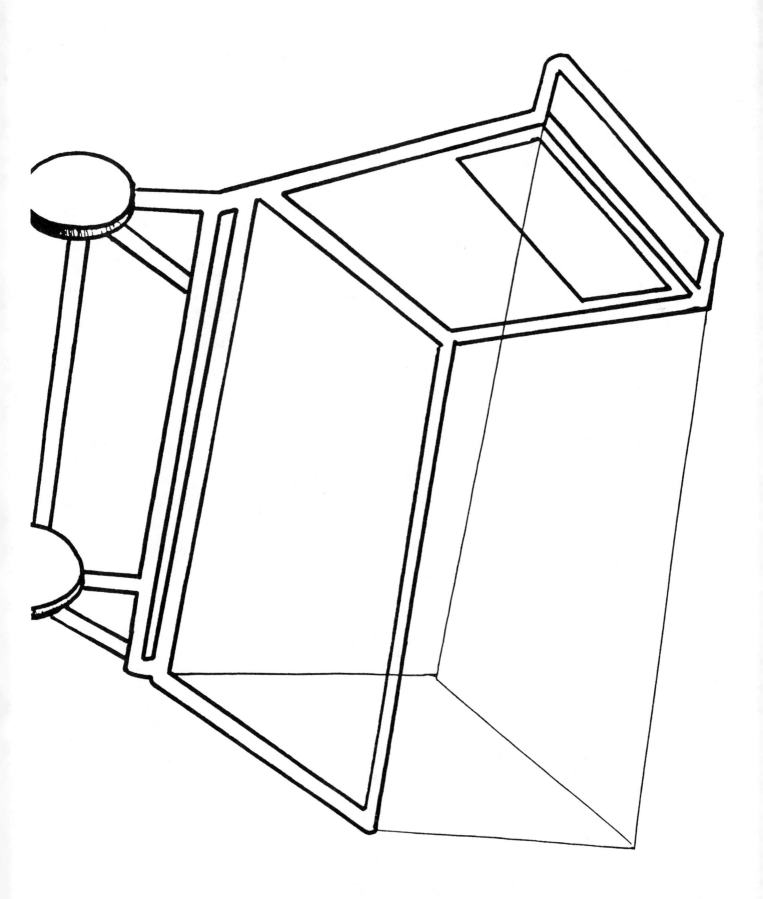

Exercise 47

THE GREAT DEBATE

Purpose:

1. To encourage one-on-one interaction.
2. To explore the dynamics of shared task completion.
3. To promote an understanding and acceptance of different points of view.

Materials:

One photocopy of the illustration for each member; pencils.

Description:

A. The group leader asks members to discuss the difference between a debate and an argument.
B. While handing out the materials, group members think of topics of interest that may be controversial. For example: curfews for people in a residential setting; the need for privacy; separate bathrooms for staff.
C. Members are paired up. They choose a topic to debate.
D. Each pair decides who will be for and who will argue against each topic. They list the reasons in their word balloons.

Group Discussion:

Each pair presents their debate to the group. Other members are encouraged to ask questions of the debaters. Members may add to either side of the debate.

If desired, the group can vote on who presented the strongest case and give reasons for their vote.

Members describe how they felt about the one-on-one interaction required in this exercise.

During discussion, the leader should take an active role in helping members avoid possible conflicts. This exercise is designed for well-integrated groups whose members are able to think abstractly.

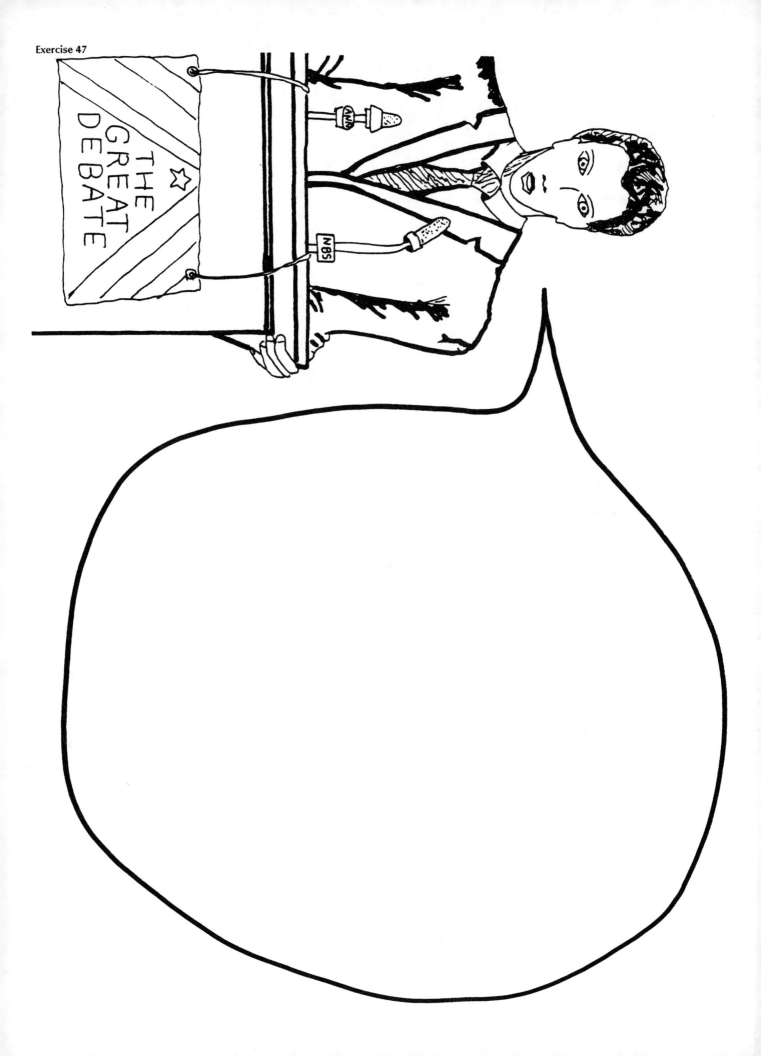

Exercise 48

MIRROR

Purpose:

1. To present risk-taking as a way of building trust.
2. To develop group cohesion through self-disclosure.
3. To promote introspection and insight.

Materials:

One photocopy of the illustration for each group member; crayons or markers.

Description:

A. The initial discussion focuses on how the image we present to others may differ from who we really are.
B. While handing out materials, the group leader instructs members to imagine a mirror which reveals their true selves.
C. Each person is given the illustration and told to draw "the real me" in the mirror, and the "me" others see on the reverse side of the page.

Group Discussion:

Each member presents the "me" others see on the reverse side of the page. The group is encouraged to discuss whether they agree with this perception. Then the real "me" in the mirror is presented by the member. The group gives feedback about the person's self-evaluation, and explores whether this gives a better understanding of who the person is.

Members generally show support and empathy for one another. This may help members to feel better about themselves and to become more trusting of each other.

This exercise is designed for groups that are well-integrated and able to think abstractly.

Variation:

Members draw in the mirror how they would like to change their physical appearance. The group discussion focuses on whether the quality of their life would improve because of this change.

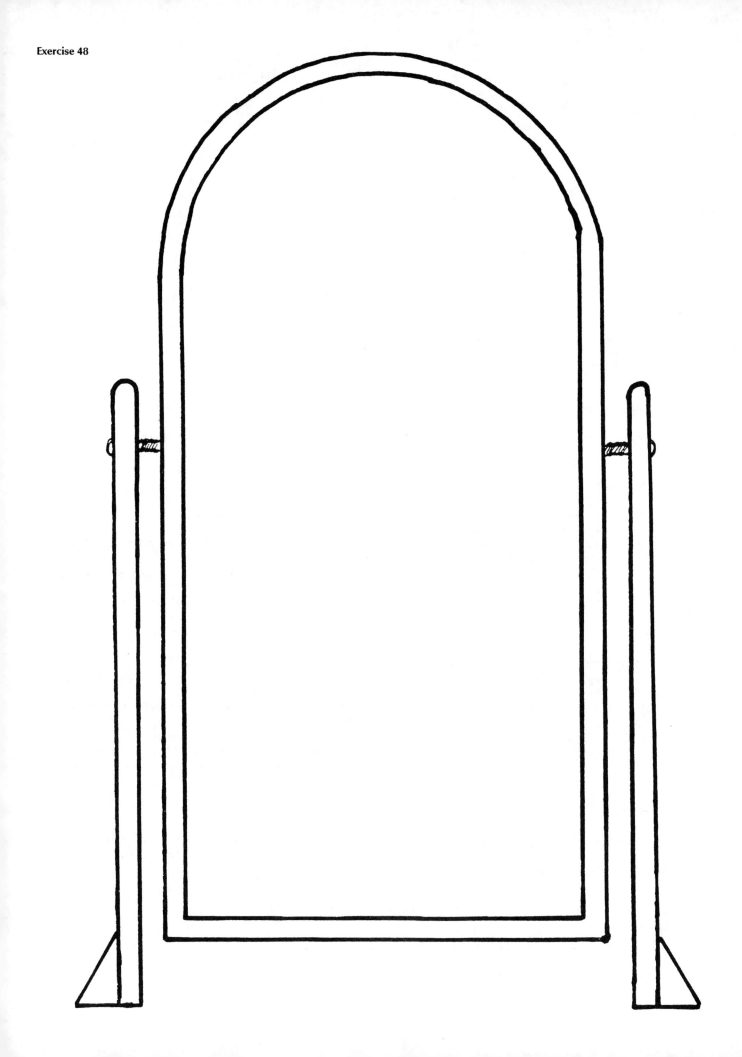

Exercise 49

RUNNING AWAY

Purpose:

1. To provide an opportunity to clarify feelings about fears.
2. To encourage empathy in order to better understand each other's needs.
3. To explore the universality of fear.

Materials:

One photocopy of the illustration for each member; crayons or markers.

Description:

A. The leader begins the exercise by encouraging members to talk about how fears can be real or imagined.
B. The materials are distributed, and the leader asks members to think about how the illustration might relate to this theme.
C. Members are told to draw in what the person in the illustration is running away from.

Group Discussion:

Members describe their illustrations to the group, and tell what it is about their particular idea that makes them fearful. The rest of the group is encouraged to explore this and offer suggestions on how to better cope with fear.

Members may concentrate on situations they share in common which may make them fearful.

This discussion may evolve into the sharing of feelings about why people experience fear.

This exercise can be interpreted on many levels, and is useful with a variety of groups.

Exercise 50

TELEVISION SCREEN

Purpose:

1. To explore common needs in order to promote group identity and cohesion.
2. To provide an opportunity for open communication and the expression of negative feelings.

Materials:

One photocopy of the illustration for each group member; crayons or markers.

Description:

A. The leader asks members to recall and discuss any news program that has reported negative aspects of institutional life.
B. While handing out the materials, participants are told to pretend there is a special television program about their own residence or facility.
C. They are then told to draw on the illustration of the television screen anything about their residence or facility that makes them angry or upset.

Group Discussion:

The leader asks members to describe what their TV program reveals about their residence or facility. The leader encourages feedback when each illustration is presented. It is important to explore the reasons behind the feelings they express.

This exercise helps members to express opinions in an accepting environment. The group can examine whether they can offer suggestions to help change any of the conditions described. This exercise is effective with groups that share a common setting.

Exercise 51

THE DASH BOARD

Purpose:

1. To explore fantasies in order to promote heightened awareness of self and others.
2. To encourage one-on-one interaction in a nonthreatening manner.
3. To experience the dynamics of shared task completion.

Materials:

One photocopy of the illustration for each team; crayons or markers.

Description:

A. The leader initiates a discussion of the pros and cons of traveling somewhere with a companion.
B. The group is divided into teams of two or three members. Each team is given the illustration.
C. Team members first talk among themselves, decide where they would like to drive, and agree on one item they would bring on the trip. They also decide who is to be the passenger(s) and who will be the driver.
D. Each team illustrates themselves, the item taken along, and their destination.

Group Discussion:

Each team shares its drawing with the other group members. The leader asks each team to explain how and why they chose the driver, the passenger(s), the item taken, and their destination.

The team is then asked to discuss feelings about working on this project together.

This exercise is both entertaining and revealing. It is useful during the early stages of group development, because it provides an opportunity for a nonthreatening form of one-on-one interaction.

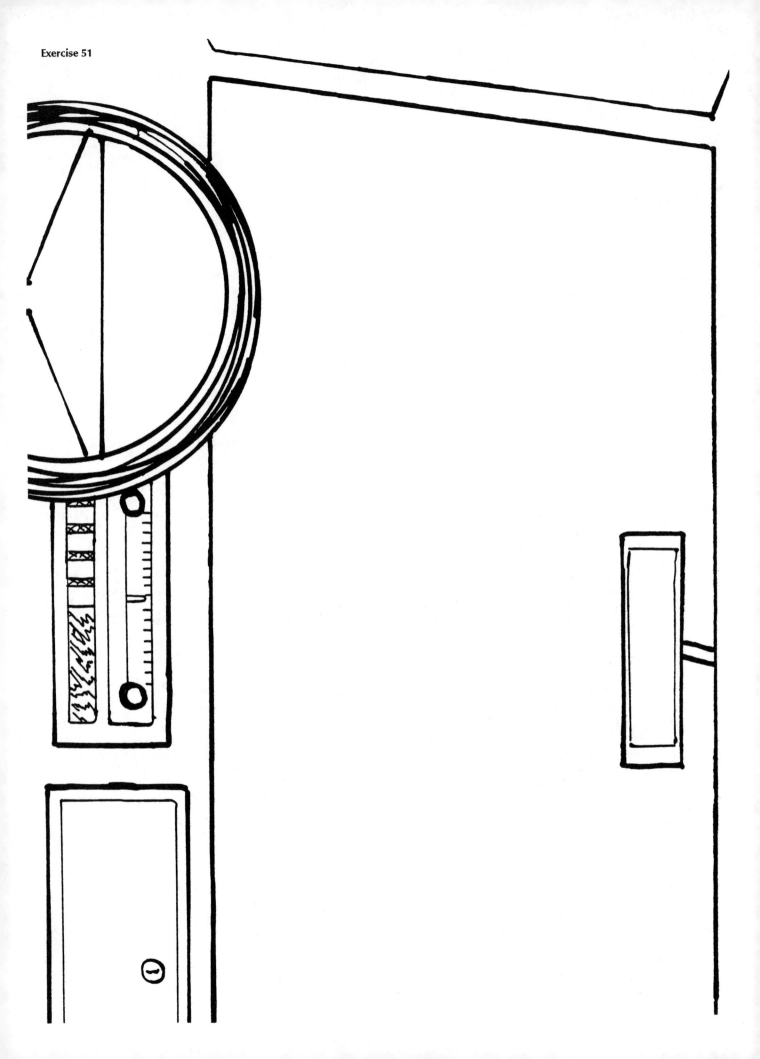

Exercise 52

ALL THE WORLD'S A STAGE

Purpose:

1. To reveal an ideal self-image through fantasy.
2. To incorporate feedback into self-evaluation.
3. To express the significance of other people in one's life through the assignment of roles.

Materials:

One photocopy of the illustration for each group member; crayons or markers.

Description:

A. The initial discussion focuses on how being a stage performer often reveals an idealized image which we would like to project to others.
B. Participants are given the illustration of the theatre and stage. They are told to draw a scene in which they would like others to see them.
C. They illustrate themselves on stage dressed in any costume they choose. Fellow group members may be included in the scene as supporting players.
D. Group members then draw the people they would like to have watching them from the audience.
E. In the VIP box, group members draw famous people who have come to see them perform.
F. Fold the page on the dotted line so that the illustration can stand upright.

Group Discussion:

Each member is asked his or her reasons for roles, costumes, and choice of supporting players. The significance of the scene which has been illustrated is explored as well.

Additionally, members are asked to give the rationale behind their choice of people, viewing them from the audience and in the VIP box, and the importance of these people in their lives.

This exercise is designed for groups which are able to think abstractly, and it may lead to additional insight.

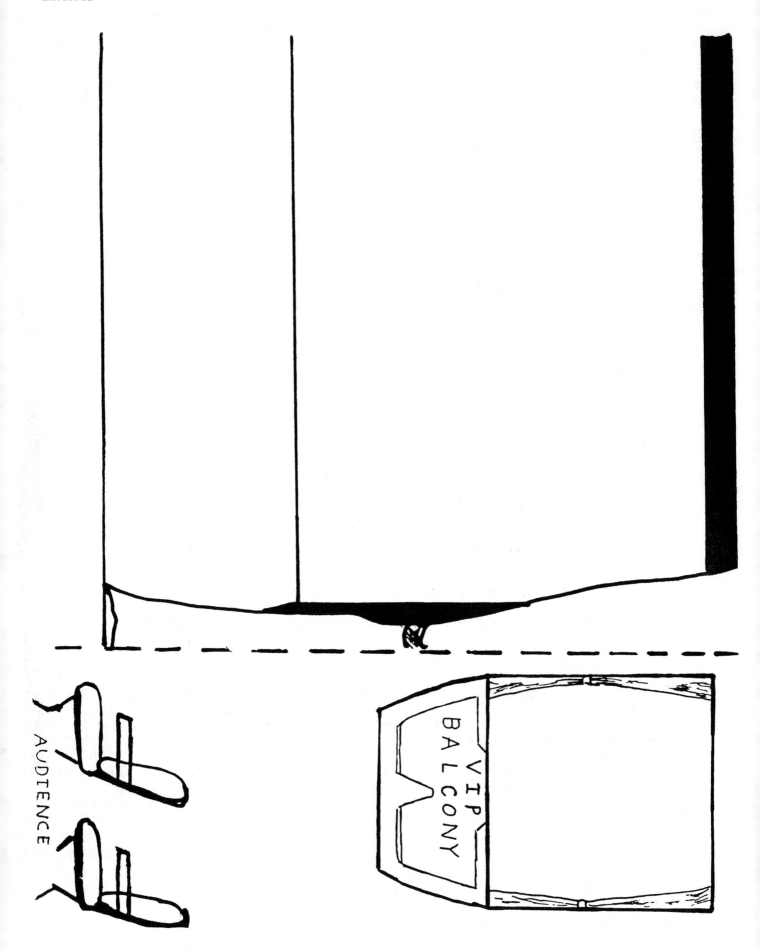

Now there are **THREE** Volumes of *Creative Therapy*!

Please send me:

_____ Copies of *Creative Therapy: 52 Exercises for Groups*
_____ Copies of *Creative Therapy II: 52 More Exercises for Groups*
_____ Copies of *Creative Therapy III: 52 More Exercises for Groups*
(<u>List Price</u>: $21.95 each. Please add shipping noted below.*)

<u>*Shipping Charges</u>
Up to $15.00 Order, Add $3.00 in US, $5.00 Foreign
$15 - $29.99 Order, Add $3.50 in US, $5.50 Foreign
$30 - $44.99 Order, Add $4.00 in US, $6.00 Foreign
$45 - $59.99 Order, Add $4.25 in US, $6.25 Foreign
Orders over $60, Add 7% in US, 10% Foreign
(Call for charges for 1, 2, or 3 day US delivery or Foreign air)

All orders from individuals and private institutions must be prepaid in full. Florida residents, add 7% sales tax. Prices and availability subject to change without notice.

For fastest service (purchase and credit card orders only)
CALL TOLL FREE 1-800-443-3364
Weekdays 9:00 - 5:00 Eastern Time
or
FAX 1-941-366-7971
24 hours a day

Check or money order enclosed (US funds only) $_____

Charge my (circle):   Visa   MasterCard   American Express   Discover

Card #_____

Exp. Date_____   Daytime Phone # (_____)_____

Signature_____

Please fold on this line and the solid line below, tape (DO NOT STAPLE), and mail.

☐ Order enclosed (ship to name and address below).

☐ Please add my name to your mailing list and send me your latest catalog.
(If you ordered this copy from Professional Resource Exchange, your name is already on our Preferred-Customer Mailing List.)

Name _____

Address _____

Address _____

City/State/Zip _____

I am a ____ psychologist; ____ clinical social worker; ____ marriage & family therapist; ____mental health counselor; ____school psychologist; ____ psychiatrist; ____other: _____

THANK YOU!

Please fold on this line and the solid line above, tape (DO NOT STAPLE), and mail.

Please cut along dotted line, fold along solid lines, and tape.